Key Terms in Ethics

Continuum *Key Terms in Philosophy*

The *Key Terms* series offers undergraduate students clear, concise and accessible introductions to core topics. Each book includes a comprehensive overview of the key terms, concepts, thinkers and texts in the area covered and ends with a guide to further resources.

Available now:

Key Terms in Logic, edited by Jon Williamson and Federica Russo
Key Terms in Philosophy of Mind, Pete Mandik
Key Terms in Philosophy of Religion, Raymond VanArragon

Key Terms in Philosophy forthcoming from Continuum:

Aesthetics, Brent Kalar
Political Philosophy, Jethro Butler

Key Terms in Ethics

Oskari Kuusela

continuum

Continuum International Publishing Group

The Tower Building
11 York Road
London SE1 7NX

80 Maiden Lane
Suite 704
New York, NY 10038

www.continuumbooks.com

British Library Cataloguing-in-Publication Data
A catalogue record for this book is available from the British Library.

ISBN: HB: 978-1-4411-6610-4
       PB: 978-1-4411-3146-1

Library of Congress Cataloging-in-Publication Data
Kuusela, Oskari.
Key terms in ethics / Oskari Kuusela.
    p. cm.
Includes index.
ISBN-13: 978-1-4411-6610-4
ISBN-10: 1-4411-6610-6
ISBN-13: 978-1-4411-3146-1 (pbk.)
ISBN-10: 1-4411-3146-9 (pbk.)
1. Ethics. 2. Ethics–Terminology. I. Title.
BJ1031.K88 2010
170–dc22   2010010414

Typeset by Newgen Imaging Systems Pvt Ltd, Chennai, India
Printed and bound in India by Replika Press Pvt Ltd

For Tuula-Liisa and Timo

Contents

Acknowledgments

Many people have helped me in one way or another to complete this book. Thanks are due to students at the University of East Anglia (UEA) who attended my courses on moral philosophy in 2007–2009, where part of the material in the book was developed and tested. Colleagues at UEA have also read some of the chapters, and I would like to thank Angela Breitenbach, Tom Greaves, Rupert Read and especially Cathy Osborne for their help. I'm very grateful to Pekka Väyrynen for his detailed comments on certain chapters as well as to Ben Walker who read through the whole manuscript and helped in improving the language. My gratitude also extends to people not involved in the process of writing in an academic capacity. They have had to endure the process or otherwise made it possible for me to devote my time to writing: Venla, Urho and Alma, and not least Angela, Anu, Despoina, Christina, Timo V., thank you so very much for your support. The au pairs Tuuli Arjovuo, Emmi Varjola and Henna Kolehmainen deserve special thanks. Finally, I am indebted to Sarah Campbell and Tom Crick at Continuum for their helpfulness and patience , as well as to the editorial team at Newgen Imagining Systems for a smooth editing process.

I dedicate this book to my parents, Tuula-Liisa and Timo Kuusela with gratitude.

Introduction

This book is written as an introduction to moral philosophy and as a reference book that provides concise accounts of central philosophical debates and issues, concepts, thinkers and works. It is designed to help the reader orient him- or herself in the field of contemporary moral philosophy, while bearing in mind that current debates and positions invariably have a history, of which it is important to be aware. Indeed, unlike in the case of the sciences, it's not clear that very significant progress has been made in moral matters since the days of Socrates. If so, what the Ancients have to say about these issues may still be directly relevant, while this might not be the case, for example, with Aristotle's physics or biology both of which are perhaps now mostly of historical interest.

The first chapter of the book introduces key concepts, distinctions, debates problems and positions. This sketch of moral philosophical discourse is complemented in the second chapter by a discussion of selected key thinkers who are either founders of schools or have otherwise influenced thinking about morality. The third chapter introduces a selection of key works from Ancient Greece to the present day. I have had to exclude many issues, thinkers and works that would have deserved discussion. This is a necessity when writing a book of this size. Nevertheless, I hope my selection is helpful and representative of discussions and positions in Western moral philosophical thinking. Perhaps slightly untypical for an introductory book is my emphasis on methodological matters relating to the aspirations, form and assumptions of moral philosophical thinking. But I consider it of the foremost importance to attend to such things explicitly, rather than tacitly accepting various methodological commitments. We shouldn't first do philosophy in a certain way and only then think about the question of whether it can beneficially be done in that way. After each section (with some exceptions) further reading is listed, in order for the reader to follow up discussions on the topic.

The individual entries or sections include many cross-references to other sections where connected issues are discussed. To follow such references in a criss-cross manner is therefore one natural way of reading the book. (If you're wondering where to start such a reading process, the section on METHODOLOGY is as good a place as any, or perhaps some of the key thinkers or works. Internal references to key works are by book title in capitals.) Another way is simply to look up sections of interest and perhaps let the reading be guided wholly by concerns external to the book's internal logic. The book can also be read straight from cover to cover. Although this is a fine way to proceed, occasionally there might be only little connection between the contents of sections that follow each other. The index can be used for finding out where issues and thinkers that don't have a section of their own are discussed or where further discussions of some issue can be found. A list of all sections is provided before the index to help the reader get an overview of the book.

I shall not try to say anything introductory about moral philosophy or its concerns and problems in this introduction. If discussion of such issues seems a helpful place to start, I recommend sections on APPLIED ETHICS, METAETHICS and NORMATIVE ETHICS. It is noteworthy, however, that moral philosophy is a peculiar field in the sense that philosophers don't really even agree on the formulation of the central questions it should address. For the Ancients the question was how one should live, of which Socrates said that life without the relevant kind of examination isn't even worth living. The Moderns transformed that into a question about what one ought to do, that is, how to act in particular situations. The way the Moderns try to answer that question is quite different from Socrates' approach: the answer isn't to be found through self-examination (to simplify a little the case of Kant) but by establishing principles that enable one to determine how to act and that can be used to justify moral judgements and relevant practices. Thus, their approach has a legislative dimension that contrasts with the Ancient's emphasis on self-knowledge. To begin the reading from such issues, the sections on PERFECTIONISM, DEONTOLOGICAL, CONSEQUENTIALIST and VIRTUE ETHICS, or sections on KANT, Mill's UTILITARIANISM, ARISTOTLE and SOCRATES offer an entrance point.

The Key Terms

Applied ethics

That philosophy should have practical relevance in the sense of enabling one to see clearly what is right or wrong or good or bad, and to live a good life, is one of its oldest aspirations. This aspiration was a central motive for Socrates who sought to convince his interlocutors that they should make the welfare of their souls their principal concern. To this end they should engage in philosophical examination of their concepts, conceptions, attitudes, and so on. (See, SOCRATES and below.) In its own way contemporary applied ethics too, as practised by analytic philosophers, is an expression of the same ambition, although philosophical activity assumes here a particular form fairly far removed from Socrates' approach. Now moral philosophy's practical relevance is understood in terms of the application of philosophical theories seeking to spell out standards or norms for morally right conduct, and thus to offer guidance for choice and action. And while the articulation of such theories is the task of NORMATIVE ETHICS, applied ethics specializes in spelling out the implications of the theories for particular practical moral issues. (See, NORMATIVE ETHICS.) Applied ethics in this sense is currently practised under the banners of all three great schools of moral philosophy – Kantian, utilitarian and virtue ethics – whereby the proponents of different theories alternatively assume as the relevant moral standard the Kantian moral law, the principle of utility or whatever a virtuous agent would do. (See, CONSEQUENTIALISM, KANT and VIRTUE ETHICS.) On this basis, arguments are then developed that purport to justify or reject actions such as abortion, euthanasia, or seek to determine principles and guidelines for the treatment of animals, our relation to the environment, and so on. Leading contemporary representatives of applied ethics include Jonathan Glover and Peter Singer.

Applied ethics in this theory-based sense emerged in the 1970s. It is partly a response to the perceived practical irrelevance of moral philosophy, as it was practised during the greater part of the twentieth century. Analytic moral philosophy at this time was mainly concerned with theoretical metaethical questions regarding the nature of morality or morally relevant language use. Metaethics in this sense was considered not to have any direct moral or normative implications. Rather, it was seen as a kind of neutral higher level or second order investigation. (The neutrality of metaethics has, of course, also been questioned. See, Metaethics.) But although it is certainly understandable to seek to change such a situation – in which moral philosophy is conceived of as practically irrelevant – to comprehend its relevance in terms of the application of theories isn't a self-evident way to understand the relevance of philosophy for moral life. Several important issues arise in response to such an account of the practical relevance of moral philosophy.

Applied ethics as the application of moral philosophical theories suggests that there might be moral experts, comparable to their scientific, medical, legal, and so on, counterparts. Such experts are people who know and understand the relevant field, theories and considerations better than others. Morality, however, seems a peculiar case when it comes to expertise. Unlike in other areas where responsibility might sometimes be delegated to experts, moral responsibility ultimately can't be delegated. When moral issues and responsibility are at stake, the agent herself is assumed to be able to judge matters for herself in the sense that, if someone consults an expert about a moral matter, acts according to the expert's advice, but things go wrong, she will still be held responsible for having believed the expert and acted on the advice. In this sense moral responsibility remains with the individual and can't be transferred to the expert as in the case of medicine, law or science. Accordingly, insofar as contemporary applied ethics assumes or encourages the conception that there are experts in moral matters to whom responsibility can be delegated, it seems to invite us onto morally problematic ground, undermining moral seriousness in the sense of taking seriously one's own responsibilities, as Lars Hertzberg has argued.

But the point, of course, isn't that philosophers shouldn't sit in committees where public policies relating to issues such as euthanasia or factory farming are discussed. In the larger context of society, general principles and guidelines of conduct seem required and moral questions relating to legislation and policies must be addressed. The contribution of philosophers to the discussion of laws and policies may well be important, insofar as they possess competence to deal with issues of high complexity, as moral matters tend to be, and comprehend the manifoldness of relevant moral considerations in connection with particular issues. The question rather concerns the relation we as moral agents should have to such principles, guidelines or policies. Once a policy of a set of rules of conduct has been established, and we have generally satisfied ourselves or its justification, are we simply to follow it without any need to worry about how things turn out morally in individual cases? Can we, in this sense, hand over our moral responsibilities to committees or moral philosophers more specifically? It seems not.

Another problem relates to the suggestion in contemporary applied ethics that mistakes in moral judgments can be understood as the expression of underlying theoretical or logical mistakes. Singer writes: '[. . .] an ethical judgment that is no good in practice must suffer from theoretical defect as well, for the whole point of ethical judgment is to guide practice.' (Singer 1993, 2) Similarly, Judith Jarvis Thomson suggests in her classic paper 'A Defence of Abortion' (in Singer 1986 ed.) that whoever infers from a foetus' right to live that a potential mother has an OBLIGATION to carry it to term is committing a logical fallacy. To this one might respond, however, that when a person finds herself pregnant and concludes she has an obligation to keep the baby, it isn't clear that this must *always* be understood as involving a logical fallacy. The agent's perception of being obliged could also be the expression of a feeling or an attitude towards the foetus to which she is perfectly entitled. Thus, although a fallacy may be involved when someone else tries to impose an obligation on a person to stay pregnant with reference to the foetus' right to live, from the first person perspective the matter seems more aptly be described as requiring the agent to search her heart, and to get clear about her attitudes and feelings. Crucial as clarity about the logic of moral expressions abstractly conceived is, it doesn't exhaust the moral issue. The approach represented by Singer and Thomson seems then problematic in the sense that to assume that our mistaken judgments are always the result of theoretical or logical mistakes is to direct our attention in a particular direction, namely, away from the agent's moral attitudes, for example, shortcomings, such as selfishness, laziness, shallowness, unjust biases, prejudices, and so on. Yet, it may often be just such shortcomings that result in her failure to understand and respond to a moral situation appropriately, and lead the agent to construe such situations, for instance, in ways all too convenient to herself.

A useful contrast can be drawn between the Socratic approach and the theory-based conception of applied ethics. The Socratic approach might be characterized as aiming at self-knowledge in the sense that the goal of the philosophical examination is that the agent achieve a clearer understanding of her own commitments (her concepts and conceptions) as well as her own attitudes (fears, hopes, desires, and so on). The purpose is, so to speak, to remove obstacles that prevent the agent from seeing things as they are, and from acting as she morally ought to, whereby such obstacles may be either misunderstandings or unhelpful attitudes. The focus thus is on the individual and how to improve morally, not the articulation of action-guiding principles. (Among contemporary thinkers this approach is represented, for example, by Iris Murdoch.) The theory-based approach, by contrast, may be characterized as moralistic in that it aims to determine standards for good or right conduct which we are assumed to adhere to, being subject to moral blame if we don't. The underlying issue here is what it really means to partake in the discussion of moral issues or to be concerned with leading a moral life. Should that be seen as necessarily involving self-examination or is it enough to adhere to principles established by experts or rely on views derived from such standards? Or, as the question might also be put: how to understand the role of action-guiding principles on the one hand, and the need for self-examination on the other, and how to reconcile these elements of moral deliberation?

Further reading

Glover, J. (1990), *Causing Death and Saving Lives*. London: Penguin.

Hertzberg, L. (2002), 'Moral Escapism and Applied Ethics'. *Philosophical Papers*, 31, (3), 251–270.

Singer, P. (ed.) (1986), *Applied Ethics*. Oxford: Oxford University Press.

Singer, P. (1993), *Practical Ethics*. Cambridge: Cambridge University Press.

Care

The concept of care has been evoked to challenge the conception of morality, moral deliberation and agency characteristic of modern moral philosophy, as exemplified by deontological and consequentialist theories. (*See*, DEONTO-LOGICAL ETHICS, CONSEQUENTIALISM.) According to this modern conception, moral thinking is based on the employment of universal moral principles that determine the obligations and RIGHTS of moral agents, whereby a key feature of moral thought is IMPARTIALITY achieved through reliance upon such principles. (*See*, IMPARTIALITY, OBLIGATION, UNIVERSALIZABILITY.) In the context of this debate, care is often contrasted with JUSTICE and acting according to the principles of justice. By contrast to justice, care is seen as involving as a crucial component the recognition of the particularity of the other person and characterized by directedness and responsiveness towards particular individuals. A care-relation therefore isn't a relation to another person in an abstract sense of a rational being, a representative of humanity, or a being with interests and desires, to whom equal and fair treatment is owed. Although it might not be necessary to hold that all questions of justice are wholly exhausted by considerations relating to the principles of justice, I adopt this simplified conception of justice here for the convenience of exposition. (*See*, JUSTICE.)

The origins of the debate surrounding care and its significance to morality and moral philosophy are in psychological studies regarding moral development and moral reasoning, and more specifically, in a dispute between Lawrence Kohlberg and Carol Gilligan in the 1970s and 1980s. An abstract justice-based orientation that Kohlberg had described as morally mature was found by Gilligan in her studies as biased against a care-based moral orientation characteristically represented by female persons. On this basis she argued for the recognition of such a different orientation or a 'different voice'. According to her, the justice-based orientation needs to be complemented by the recognition of the care-based orientation as being of equal importance, and by acknowledging that considerations of care and responsibility within personal relationships are an irreducible element of morality. In this way, she suggests, the bias of traditional moral philosophy against characteristically (though not exclusively) female approaches to morality can be corrected.

Subsequently, the concept of care has been employed as the basis of accounts of morality, especially in the so-called feminist ethics where it plays a central role. (Feminist ethics as such is a broader set of approaches, involving, for example, Marxist, existentialist, psychoanalytic, postcolonial, ecological and other schools.) Rather than an affirmation of the traditional role of females as carers and their place in the private sphere of home, however, care is often argued by care-ethicists to be able to also explain the notion of justice, and to constitute in this sense the foundation of morality as a whole, including both private and public spheres. Arguments to this effect are presented, for example, by Nel Noddings and Michael Slote. But whether one of the concepts of justice or care should be seen as *the* fundamental one, and whether morality is a unitary phenomenon explainable by reference to something that could be regarded as *the* essence or *the* core of it, isn't clear, as Lawrence Blum emphasizes. (*See also*, METHODOLOGY.) Accordingly, Gilligan, for example, regards justice and care as different aspects of morality, neither of which is reducible to the other, though she demonstrates a potentially problematic tendency to regard the two in a dualistic manner. Virginia Held too holds that neither care nor justice can be explained in terms of the other without losing sight of what is distinctive to each. According to her areas where each has priority should be delineated, though neither is confined to either the private or public sphere. She conceives of care as having a priority in the sense that caring relations constitute a wider framework into which justice is to be fitted, albeit 'fitting' here doesn't mean reduction. (For the notion of reduction, *see* NATURALISM AND NON-NATURALISM.) In particular, she envisages care as fundamental in the sense that without care there wouldn't be anything else, including justice, because life and its continuity require care. According to Held, ethics of care is a distinct moral theory or approach to moral theorizing, not something that can be added on or included in approaches such as Kantian, utilitarian or virtue ethics. By contrast, Slote, although he too regards care ethics as inconsistent with Kantianism and as capable of providing a comprehensive account of both individual and political morality, has argued that care ethics is part of VIRTUE ETHICS. Here caring emerges as the primary virtue and motive for action. Against this Held maintains that, unlike in virtue ethics, the focus of care ethics isn't the agent's character but rather caring relations. (*See*, VIRTUE ETHICS.)

As for the notion of care itself, it is often characterized as something distinct both from the objective and subjective or the impersonal and purely personal. When caring for someone, the carer isn't concerned with simply her own personal interests. Rather, care involves a relation to a particular other in the sense that it requires attentiveness to the needs of this particular person and to her particularity. In this sense it isn't a matter of acting to the benefit of sentient beings generally or out of respect for humanity in an abstract sense, as utilitarianism and Kantian ethics see moral action. In the latter respect care, then, isn't anything impersonal either and objective in this sense of abstraction from particular interests. As Held explains, carers seek to promote a relationship between them and particular others. Caring (by contrast to providing a service) is a relationship where the carer and the cared-for share an interest in their mutual well-being. Accordingly, instead of assuming a conception of persons as separate, self-sufficient and independent individuals (as traditional ethics, commonly spelt out by males has tended to do), care ethics assumes a relational conception that regards persons as interdependent. Or as Held also says, while justice protects equality and FREEDOM, care fosters social bonds and cooperation. Here the values of trust, solidarity, mutual concern and empathetic responsiveness have priority, rather than IMPARTIALITY, fairness of distribution and non-interference. In this connection, attentiveness is important also in the sense that attending to the other person's needs, and understanding what they really are, is what prevents the carer from imposing her own conception of the good on the other person.

Another characteristic feature of care ethics is its valuing of emotion. In particular, care ethics seeks to promote the cultivation of EMOTIONS such as sympathy, empathy, sensitivity and responsiveness. Importantly, this isn't merely understood as a help for implementing the moral dictates of reason, but rather the development of relevant emotional sensitivities is seen as a way to better ascertain what morality requires. Accordingly, Gilligan maintains that morality necessarily involves the intertwining of emotion, cognition and action. (*See also*, EMOTIONS.) Slote has argued in this regard that the basis of care ethics is the feeling of empathy, connecting care ethics with the sentimentalism of Lord Shaftesbury (1671–1713), Francis Hutcheson (1694–1746), Adam Smith (1723–1790) and David Hume, in whose thinking he takes the care approach to originate. (*See*, HUME.) Slote's comparison seems to emphasize care as a *motive*, however, which might be problematic in the sense that, as Held argues, to regard care as a motive runs the risk of losing sight of the work it involves and of care as a moral practice incorporating certain values. According to her, to characterize someone as a caring person is to characterize her as morally admirable, and in this sense the notion of caring picks out a specific valuable characteristic that persons but also societies may possess. How deep the contrast between Held and Slote runs isn't entirely clear.

Similarly, also Slote emphasizes the notion of care as providing us with a standard that can be used as the basis of moral evaluation.

The conception that the basis of ethics is a relation to a particular other is also a central theme in the work of Emmanuel Levinas. Similarly, he too addresses questions about the relation between particularity and the universal rules of justice. (*See*, Levinas.)

Further reading

Blum, L. (1994), *Moral Perception and Particularity*. Cambridge: Cambridge University Press.

Gilligan, C. (1993), *In a Different Voice: Psychological Theory and Women's Development*. Cambridge, MA: Harvard University Press.

Held, V. (2006), *The Ethics of Care: Personal, Political, and Global*. Oxford: Oxford University Press.

Slote, M. (2007), *The Ethics of Care and Empathy*. London: Routledge.

Cognitivism and non-cognitivism

A long standing dispute between the so-called cognitivists and non-cognitivists in meta-ethics concerns the nature of moral judgments. The question is, whether moral judgments are truth-apt, that is, whether they can be understood as stating something true or false about reality, and therefore have cognitive value in this sense. Cognitivists answer this question affirmatively, while the non-cognitivist answer is negative. According to the latter, the logical role of moral judgments isn't to state anything true or false, being instead the expression of attitudes of a different kind. Although philosophers may traditionally have had a tendency to adopt a cognitivist outlook, this trend changed as a consequence of G. E. Moore's famous open-question argument (*see, PRINCIPIA ETHICA*). Although Moore himself was a cognitivist, in the wake of his argument non-cognitivism became the dominant theory in twentieth-century analytical moral philosophy until the 1960s or 1970s. Other questions related to the issue of the truth-aptness of moral judgments include the following. If moral judgments are true or false, what are they true or false about? Are there moral properties and facts? If so, what kind of properties or facts are they? Are moral judgments objective? If they are objective what does their objectivity mean? Notably, although most cognitivists are realists, these positions are not identical. For example, although Kant presumably assumes that there is moral knowledge, his position isn't realist in the sense that the moral law isn't determined by or read off from any facts pertaining to reality (including empirical facts about human beings). Rather, it is something we find 'inside ourselves' as rational beings. (*See, KANT.*) (Kant has sometimes also been argued to be a forerunner of non-cognitivism.)

Non-cognitivism has roots in the thought of HUME. According to him, reason as such doesn't allow us to recognize any state of affairs as morally good or bad, but this is recognized only on the basis of a moral sense. Accordingly, Hume problematizes the assumption that one could derive statements about how things ought to be from statements about how things are, and in this sense deduce moral judgments from beliefs concerning facts. Moral judgments are not true or false, but to be regarded as the expression of moral sentiments. (*See, HUME.*) More recently, moral properties and facts have been argued to be ontologically 'queer' (in J. L. Mackie's expression) in the sense that they are supposed to have the characteristic of necessitating certain actions. But, as the puzzle is spelt out, how could any fact or belief in the obtaining of a fact necessitate on its own any kind of action? For example, even if the fact that a house is on fire might seem to give reason to leave the house and alert others to do so, it may be argued that this isn't really so. To constitute a reason to leave the house the recognition of the fact must be combined with a desire not to be burnt by fire and that others shouldn't be consumed by fire. On the basis of considerations of this type, Mackie concludes in his argument from queerness that moral judgments are always false. Moral value is not a real quality of actions, for example, and nothing in the world corresponds to moral concepts. This view of the universal falsity of moral judgments is the basis of his so-called error theory.

As Mackie's argument suggests, non-cognitivism appears to have certain advantages. Given that non-cognitivists don't regard moral judgments as statements about reality, they are immediately released from answering difficult questions relating to the ontology of value that cognitivists must answer. Non-cognitivists, however, face other issues. For example, they need to explain the apparent rationality of moral discourse and the appearance that moral judgment can be correct or incorrect. Let's first look at some examples of non-cognitivist theories and thereafter cognitivist alternatives.

According to emotivism, represented by C. L. Stevenson and Alfred Ayer, ethical terms don't add anything to the content or literal meaning of our statements. For example, 'You acted wrong in stealing that money' means just the same as 'You stole that money'. The only difference is the emotion of moral disapproval expressed by the first sentence. It is as if saying 'You stole the money' with a 'peculiar tone of horror' or as if it were written with additional exclamation marks, as Ayer puts it (Ayer 1946/2001, 110). In this sense, moral judgments are to be regarded as the expression of the speaker's feelings of approval or disapproval, perhaps intended to stimulate certain actions. Thus, the function of ethical terms is emotive, and ethical judgments have no objective validity.

Emotivism has the consequence that, despite appearances, there are no genuine ethical disputes. Two people who express different moral sentiments are not really contradicting each other because neither is making a true/false assertion. According to Ayer, to the extent that moral disputes are genuine disputes, they are disputes about facts. A moral argument is an attempt to show that someone is mistaken about the facts, for example, relating to a particular action. Such an argument is based on the assumption that normally anyone who has had a similar moral education would have the same attitude towards said action, if they knew the facts. In cases where arguments about facts can't solve the matter, however, we must declare the case insoluble. (But *see also*, EMOTIONS.)

Richard M. Hare's universal prescriptivism is partly designed to avoid the irrationalism of emotivism. A central feature of Hare's theory is his distinction between the so-called descriptive and prescriptive meaning and the idea that moral judgments combine these two kinds of elements. (See also, THICK AND THIN MORAL CONCEPTS.) Descriptive meaning is something they share with factual judgments. This makes moral judgments universalizable, which depends on the concept of similarity or sameness. If I describe an object as an x, then I must call any relevantly similar object 'x' on pain of inconsistency. The same goes for moral judgments, given that they have descriptive meaning. By contrast, imperatives are not universalizable: someone who gives an order isn't committed to giving the same order when the same circumstances occur again. (*See*, UNIVERSALIZABILITY.)

As regards prescriptive meaning, when making the judgment that someone is a good man, Hare explains, we don't merely say that it is right to call him 'good'. Rather, we are also prescribing this man for imitation. Similarly, to characterize an action as right or good is to prescribe or command it as something that ought to be done. It isn't possible, however, to derive the prescriptive meaning of a statement from its descriptive meaning. People may agree on the descriptive meaning of a term but differ about its prescriptive meaning, which possibility shows, Hare maintains, that there are indeed two such elements contained in a moral judgment. Universal prescriptivism can now be defined as a theory according to which: moral judgments are (1) universalizable, (2) prescriptive, and (3) possess descriptive meaning. That moral judgments have these characteristics, Hare thinks, is sufficient to establish the rationality of morals and the possibility of moral arguments. (For example, moral judgment-making can now be said to require consistency, while it is unclear on what basis this could be demanded of the expression of emotion.) Universalization also provides a test for the acceptability of the prescription. Unless a prescription can be universalized, it can't be said to be something we morally ought to do.

Expressivism, developed by Simon Blackburn, too explains moral judgments as the expression of human's moral sentiments. An aspect of this theory is a non-realist explanation of moral necessity and OBLIGATION according to which, rather than being grounded on facts, such necessities and obligations are a projection of our sentiments onto reality. Consequently, such necessities can then also become the object of discussion and knowledge claims. In this way Blackburn seeks to explain the appearance that there are truths, for example, about moral obligations. But although he regards moral necessity as dependent on our attitudes, Blackburn denies that his theory is a form of conventionalism, according to which we can simply decide to establish a convention that such and such is morally necessary. What it means for x to be forbidden or wrong (and so on) is for us to have such and such attitudes towards it. That we have such and such attitudes towards it, however, isn't what *makes* x forbidden or wrong.

To turn now to cognitivist theories, they too come in many forms. The general idea is that moral judgments are to be understood as true or false statements, or that they can be explained in terms of such statements. But what the truth or falsity of moral judgments depends on, or what makes them true or false and what their cognitive content is, is understood in many ways by different philosophers. For example, Moore takes goodness to be a non-natural property of natural objects known through intuition, whereby intuition is thought to provide us with knowledge of whether objects possess this property. This kind of intuitionism, however, is often criticized for leaving the nature of moral knowledge mysterious. (*See, PRINCIPIA ETHICA* and NATURALISM AND NON-NATURALISM.)

A representative of cognitivism who significantly contributed to its return to the philosophical scene is Philippa Foot. In her early articles (from the 1950s) she takes issue with non-cognitivists such as Hare, one of her objections being that his account of morality can't really explain its rationality. In the light of Hare's theory, Foot maintains, the choice of moral principles (or choice about what kind of life to lead) emerges as a mere matter of decision and preference that can't be grounded by any argument. That is, while the UNIVERSALIZABILITY requirement imposes a requirement of consistency on moral judgments *after* the choice of moral principles has been decided, initially there are no restrictions for their choice, as long as one treats them as universal. There is, therefore, no justification for moral principles beyond the agents' preferences or desires and, consequently, it is always possible for moral arguments to break down, even when people engaged in the argument agree on all the facts. It suffices for the insolublility of disagreement that the disputing persons subscribe to different moral principles.

Behind this lies Hare's (Humean) assumption that descriptions of facts, or the descriptive meanings of statements, are evaluatively entirely neutral, and that there are no objective relations between facts and values, or no logical connection between statements of fact and statements of value. This gap between fact and value means that one can never explain, for example, the wrongness of an action by reference to facts pertaining to it. Nothing in the action itself makes it morally good or bad. This is what Foot wants to deny. She asks: Is it really correct that descriptive premises never entail or count as evidence for an evaluative conclusion? Is it always possible to assert a descriptive premise and deny an evaluative conclusion? Foot's counter-example is the description of someone's action as rude. It seems that, at least sometimes, such a description is a ground for a negative moral evaluation. (Here it is important that not just anything can be called 'rude' or described as rude, unless one abandons the ways we normally describe and talk about things. But while the latter is possible, such descriptions have no bearing on the issue of whether 'rude', as it is normally used, sometimes entails a negative evaluation.) If Foot's point about rudeness is correct, she has a counter-argument to the idea that descriptions are necessarily value neutral and that descriptions can only lead to an evaluative conclusion when connected with a moral principle that has no logical connection with facts. This constitutes at the same time a counter-argument to Hare's view that we can always disagree about moral conclusions even though we agree on all the facts. (*See*, THICK AND THIN MORAL CONCEPTS.)

Another influential cognitivist is John McDowell whose cognitivism, unlike Foot's, is non-naturalistic. (*See*, NATURALISM AND NON-NATURALISM.) McDowell too criticizes the non-cognitivist notion of the purely descriptive as problematic. According to him, the non-cognitivist view of the disentangling of the descriptive and evaluative presupposes that it is possible to classify, for example, actions in a way that corresponds to a classification in terms of an evaluative concept such as courageous, on the basis of the actions' descriptive properties alone. Thus, non-cognitivism presupposes that the extension of an evaluative concept (i.e. the cases to which it can be applied) could be understood without understanding the relevant evaluation. This McDowell takes to be impossible.

McDowell also argues against the view that the objectivity in moral evaluation would require, as Hare's conception of descriptive meaning as the basis of the objectivity of moral judgments assumes, that we are able to comprehend whatever our evaluations concern independently of an evaluative point of view. Objectivity doesn't require in this sense, McDowell argues, that we should abstract from sensitivities and capacities relevant for the application of moral concepts. Rather, as the objectivity of practices of rule-following, for instance, in mathematics shows, objectivity is a feature of statements within certain conceptual practices. McDowell compares value judgments to statements about colour. Just as the experience of colour depends on certain subjective sensitivities, so the experience of value presupposes one being initiated in certain practices and having developed a required kind of a perceptive capacity or sensitivity. The objectivity of moral judgments therefore stands in similarity to the objectivity of colour statements.

Such considerations then lead us, according to McDowell, to a form of cognitivism according to which moral properties are properties out there in the world, like colours are, and thus make demands on our reason. Like colour concepts, moral concepts pick out patterns in the world which are not identifiable independently of the relevant concepts and the classifications they are employed to express. Consequently, what a situation morally requires can be grasped correctly or incorrectly, but there is no explanation of our moral concepts and practices from a perspective external to morality and in non-moral terms.

In addition to the positions discussed here there are a multitude of cognitivist and non-cognitivist positions as well as positions that combine elements of both, such as Mark Timmons and Terry Horgan's cognitivist expressivism. Examples of non-cognitivism include Allan Gibbard's Norm-expressivism, and examples of cognitivism various forms of reductive and non-reductive naturalistic positions. The latter are exemplified by the so-called Cornell realism represented by David Brink, Geoffrey Sayre-McCord and Nicholas Sturgeon, and the former by Frank Jackson and Philip Pettit. (*See*, NATURALISM AND NON-NATURALISM.)

Further reading

Ayer, A. (2001*), Language, Truth and Logic*. London: Penguin Books.
Hare, R. M. (1952), *The Language of Morals*. Oxford: Oxford University Press.

Horgan T. and Timmons M. (eds) (2006), *Metaethics after Moore*. Oxford: Oxford University Press.

McDowell, J. (1998), 'Values and Secondary Qualities', in *Mind, Value and Reality*. Cambridge, MA: Harvard University Press, pp. 131–150.

McNaughton, D. (1988), *Moral Vision: An Introduction to Ethics*. Oxford: Blackwell.

Miller, A. (2003), *An Introduction to Contemporary Metaethics*. Oxford: Polity Press.

Consequentialism

Consequentialist theories regard the moral value of actions, rules of conduct, and so on, as dependent on their consequences. Theories of this type may be characterized as teleological in the sense that they regard the moral value of actions and states of affairs, not as anything intrinsic to them, but as dependent on their promoting a particular external end – *telos*. This end, which conveys value to actions and states of affairs, is itself regarded as intrinsically good, or good as such, desirable for its own sake. (*See,* GOOD.) Different forms of consequentialism can be distinguished on the basis of what they regard as the end our actions ought to promote and as the source of their moral value. Examples are general happiness, welfare or interest satisfaction, and happiness or interest satisfaction conceived purely egoistically. The most influential form of consequentialism is utilitarianism which is the focus of this section. Utilitarianism itself takes different forms, as I will explain.

According to classical utilitarianism, developed by Jeremy Bentham (1784–1832) and John Stuart Mill (1806–1873), the foundation of morality, that is, the single fundamental principle on which it is based, is the utility-principle, or as Bentham called it, the Greatest Happiness principle. (*See,* UTILITARIANISM.) According to this principle, the rightness of actions depends on their tendency to promote happiness, by which Bentham and Mill understand pleasure and the absence of pain. Later writers have articulated different conceptions of utility, for example, utility as the satisfaction of desires, preferences or interests, divorcing utilitarianism from the hedonism of its early representatives. Other prominent proponents of utilitarianism include Henry Sidgwick, G. E. Moore and Hare. What remains common to utilitarians regardless of their favoured conception of utility, however, is the idea that actions – or more broadly, human practices, the organization of society, and so on – should aim at the maximization of utility. Thus, utility (or happiness or welfare) emerges as the ultimate end of conduct, the only thing that is good in itself, its maximization being the source of moral obligation. Anything else, for example virtue, is good only as a means, insofar as it contributes to the maximization of utility. Importantly, for utilitarianism the maximization of welfare, for instance, means here the maximization of welfare overall, not the maximization of the welfare of an individual, possibly at others' expense. Utilitarian morality isn't egoistic, but involves as an important component the ideal of IMPARTIALITY. (*See,* IMPARTIALITY.) The idea of the maximization of welfare may also be extended beyond humanity to cover all sentient beings who, for instance, have an interest to avoid pain.

As regards the role or status of the utility-principle, it is intended to spell out the criterion by which the rightness/wrongness of actions is determined and by reference to which actions are justified. This means that the principle need not be seen as something one should always be thinking about when deciding what to do, or that acting according to the principle should be one's explicit, conscious motive. A utilitarian is free to maintain, for example, that we should typically let our actions be guided by the principles of common-sense morality, such as 'Don't lie', or by other established rules of conduct, rather than trying to calculate, in each case, which course of action would maximize utility. As the critics of utilitarianism have pointed out, such calculations would often be cumbersome and detrimental to the purpose, for example, when a situation requires a quick response. Similarly, it seems to make a moral difference, it has been pointed out by Michael Stocker, whether my motive to visit my friend in a hospital is the thought that this is what the utility-principle generally requires or my concern for this particular person's well-being. (See also, CARE.) Ultimately, however, the moral worth and justification of principles and practices – such as the institutions of promising and friendship – is to be decided, from a utilitarian perspective, on the basis of the utility-principle which, in this sense, occupies a fundamental place in the hierarchy of moral principles. (See, OBLIGATION.)

The acknowledgement of multiple levels of moral principles (in the above sense) marks a distinction between more complex multiple-level and simpler single-level forms of utilitarianism. The advantage of the more complex view is that it can avoid criticisms that assume utilitarianism to be committed to a conception of moral thought as always involving explicit calculations of utility, or take utilitarianism to require one to be a cold person of principle solely aiming to maximize overall happiness. The latter would mean that a utilitarian couldn't, for example, appreciate friendship for its own sake, beyond its service to the utility-principle.

Another distinction between forms of utilitarianism is the distinction between act-utilitarianism and rule-utilitarianism. Whereas the former sees the moral value of an action as directly dependent on the consequences of the action itself, the latter regards the value of an action as dependent on the consequences of the adoption of a rule that prescribes how one should act in relevant kinds of circumstances. (Rule-utilitarianism is also referred to as indirect utilitarianism: it conceives of the justification of actions indirectly, by reference to relevant rules of conduct. Here the utility-principle is seen as applying, in the first instance, to rules rather than directly to actions them- selves. A rule of conduct of the relevant kind is then justified insofar as utility would be maximized if we always acted according to it.) The motivation for rule-utilitarianism is the following problem for simple, straightforward act-utilitarianism. Assuming that moral evaluations focus on the consequences of individual actions in particular circumstances, utilitarianism seems some- times to allow or even require wronging individuals or minorities, insofar as this leads to the maximization of good overall in relevant circumstances. For example, an innocent person might be sacrificed as a scapegoat to avoid unrest and the resultant loss of many lives. Rule-utilitarianism, by contrast, seems able to avoid this problem, assuming that the adoption of rules that licence injus- tices towards individuals or minorities doesn't ultimately maximize overall happiness. If so, such rules, and corresponding actions, are not justified.

A different, act-utilitarian way to respond to the problem with simple act-utilitarianism is to take into account the consequences of actions more broadly, or their general tendency to promote welfare, instead of focusing on individual actions in particular circumstances. Thus, one might argue against the justification of using an individual as a scapegoat on the grounds that allowing acts of this kind facilitates the adoption of morally problematic prac- tices or leads to the moral corruption of peoples' character, and so on. More broadly conceived, consequences such as these may also be considered as part of the consequences of an action, and an act-utilitarian need not restrict the breadth of her moral considerations by focusing exclusively on the imme- diate consequences of individual actions in specific circumstances. Notably, the act-utilitarian is also able to avoid the criticism sometimes directed against rule-utilitarianism that it constitutes a form of rule-worship. The problem is that that rule-utilitarianism requires one to stick to a rule even when deviating from it would produce the best consequences in particular circumstances, and in this sense it goes against the spirit of consequentialism.

Returning to consequentialism more generally, its focus on the consequences of actions (or of rules of conduct and practices) might be seen as an acknowledgement of the uncertainties pertaining to moral life. What consequences an action will have is an empirical matter, sometimes perhaps a matter of pure chance. Depending on whether the moral worth of an action is regarded as dependent on its actual or probable consequences, however, this uncertainty gives rise to slightly different difficulties for consequentialism. Insofar as the value of an action depends on its actual consequences, an accidentally unsuccessful murderer might turn out as worthy of moral praise by consequentialist lights, insofar as the failed attempt at murder happens to have good consequences. Equally problematically, depending on how far in the future we must look to determine the consequences of an action, consequentialism may lead to the conclusion that it is impossible to determine the moral value of any action, given difficulties about predicting the future. (Thus, Moore concludes that we can't know what our duties are; see, PRINCIPIA ETHICA.) These problems can be solved, if by consequences one understands probable consequences foreseeable by the agent. Now the unsuccessful murderer may be blamed for what she tried to achieve. This view isn't without problems of its own either, however. If the goodness of an action is determined exclusively by reference to probable consequences, its actual consequences are thereby rendered irrelevant for moral evaluation. Thus, one may have to characterize an action with unforeseeable horrific consequences as the morally right one.

Part of the appeal of utilitarianism to philosophers has been its simplicity and economy. Utilitarianism promises to explain the apparently complex phenomenon of morality by reference to one single overarching principle that constitutes the basis for all moral evaluation, and explains why things have the moral value they do. The moot question, however, is whether striving after the ideals of simplicity and economy, derived from the sciences, helps rather than hinders a clear comprehension of matters in ethics. (See, METHODOLOGY, PARTICULARISM AND GENERALISM.)

Further reading

Darwall, S. (ed.) (2003), *Consequentialism*. Oxford: Blackwell.

Glover, J. (ed.) (1990), *Utilitarianism and Its Critics*. New York: Macmillan.

Smart, J. J. C. and Williams, B. (1973), *Utilitarianism: For and Against*. Cambridge: Cambridge University Press.

Stocker, Michael (1976), 'The Schizophrenia of Modern Ethical Theories'. *Journal of Philosophy*, 76, 453–466.

Deontological ethics

The terms 'deontology', 'deontological ethics' and 'deontologism' refer to a type of moral philosophical theory that seeks to ground morality on a moral law or norm which moral agents have an OBLIGATION to conform to. Deontological ethics, in this sense, is law-based, and envisages the morally right and the good as determined through relevant norms. (The name derives from Greek '*deon*' for 'what one must do', 'what ought to be done' or 'duty'.) Deontological ethics stands in contrast with consequentialist ethics that regards moral value as dependent on the consequences of, for instance, an agent's actions. (See, CONSEQUENTIALISM.)

Deontological ethics include religious ethics that assume morality to be based on a law given to us by divine agency. (See, GOD AND RELIGION.) Such a religious conception takes the source of moral norms to be external to human beings with our duties being determined by an independent authority. On this view the moral law constitutes, in effect, a constraint on the FREEDOM of moral agents. Similarly, the Stoic conception that we ought to live in harmony with the laws of nature involves an idea of submitting to and accepting laws that are given from the outside. Whether such laws of nature should be seen as an external constraint on human FREEDOM, however, is perhaps less clear in connection with the Stoic view than on the religious conception. (See, STOIC ETHICS.) Another and perhaps the most prominent example of deontological ethics is Kant's moral philosophy. His view is distinctive, however, in that for Kant the moral law doesn't depend on any external authority. Rather, he takes our duties to be derivable from reason alone. On this view, the moral law is a law which human beings issue autonomously to themselves, and it assumes nothing but their own rationality. Accordingly, in doing our duty we are not constrained by anything external, but are rather fulfilling our own essence and freedom. This also explains how the moral law can bind us. It is binding as a law we give to ourselves. (See, KANT and *GROUNDWORK*.) Another way to explain the status and bindingness of moral norms is contractualism. This view regards our obligations as based on a contract which, in one sense or another, we have entered or can't reasonably reject. (See, Rawls' *A THEORY OF JUSTICE*.)

A key feature of deontologism as opposed to consequentialism is that, from its point of view, actions (for example) can be regarded as right or wrong as such, or intrinsically. Their value, in other words, is unconditional or absolute, not relative to any further considerations beyond what the moral law prescribes. In this sense moral value is entirely independent of any consequences an action might have. No matter how good the consequences, for example, of murdering someone might be, it ought not be done – or even considered. On the other hand, someone who does what is right simply out of duty, and not because it serves some further end (e.g. because it gives the agent a good reputation as a dutiful person, or allows her to avoid punishment), does it for its own sake.

Deontological ethics can be understood as person-relative in the sense that it may attribute different duties to different people. For example, parents may be regarded as having duties to their children, and more generally, there may be duties according to the role of a person in society or a group. To understand obligations as person-relative in this sense is also to construe reasons for action as person-relative. Thus, what might be a reason for one person to do something, need not be a reason for another person with different obligations. (More specifically, in contemporary deontology there are both so-called agent-centred and patient-centred positions. In the latter case the obligations of an agent are not determined by reference to any characteristics of the agent herself or her actions, but by the RIGHTS of the persons who are at the receiving end of her actions.) By contrast to the person-centred versions of deontology, the notion of a moral agent in Kant's ethics is extremely thin, abstracting from all particular features of individual humans. All that moral action requires, according to his view, is a will governed by reason. This, however, isn't substantial enough for distinguishing between different persons and their duties. Thus, Kantian duties are universal for all rational beings, not person-relative. (*See*, IMPARTIALITY.)

Finally, another distinction between deontological positions is the following. It is possible for a deontologist to maintain that there are a number of duties without any systematic unity, for example, duties to family or friends, duties relating to one's occupation, a duty not to steal, and so on. Such a position would not be accepted by all deontologists, however, because morality now emerges as a mere random collection of obligations without any systematicity. Such a conception also leaves no way to determine the completeness of the account of duties, unlike when assuming a systematic account. By contrast to the unsystematic view, Kant and Kantians take our moral duties to be determined by a single supreme principle that underlies the whole morality and constitutes its foundation. (*See*, KANT, METHODOLOGY, NORMATIVE ETHICS.)

Further reading

Darwall, S. (ed.) (2003), *Deontology*. Oxford: Blackwell.
Davis, N. A. (1993), 'Contemporary Deontology', in P. Singer (ed.), *A Companion to Ethics*. Oxford: Blackwell, pp. 205–218.

Emotions

The role of emotions in moral life and their significance for moral deliberation is a topic where views diverge widely. All moral philosophers and schools recognize that emotions can have some moral relevance. How this role is understood more precisely, however, depends, for instance, on whether emotions are regarded as possessing any cognitive content or as non-cognitive affective and desiderative states that we are subject to but which can also motivate and produce actions. In the latter capacity emotions might still be responsive to the deliverances of the intellect, for example, corrigible by reason, and possible to educate and cultivate. Envisaged in this way they can't, however, contribute cognitively or intellectually to our moral understanding of agents, actions or situations. While some philosophers, for example Hume, posit emotions (passions) as the foundation of morality (*see*, Hume), others such as Kant regard emotions as much too unstable for this role (*see*, Kant and *groundwork*). On the other hand, while for Kant the moral worth of an action doesn't depend on the emotions experienced by the agent (except in that overcoming emotive resistances may make an action's moral character even clearer), an Aristotelian point of view readily accommodates the agent's emotive state as something that may influence our moral perception of her. Being virtuous is also a matter of having appropriate emotions and emotional reactions. (*See*, Aristotle.)

In accordance with the latter conception, it seems clear that the emotions someone feels may affect our perception of, for instance, whether they are an admirable or a decent person. Similarly, when someone does something good but with feelings that don't suit the action, this may influence our moral evaluation, not only of the person, but also the action. For example, if an action meets the external marks of generosity but is hateful to the agent, we might not characterize it as genuinely generous. Emotions themselves, or lack thereof, also seem a possible object of moral evaluation, as in the case of disapproving of the racist hatred someone feels or when a person fails to feel regret or shame for what she has done. In ways such as these an agent's expression of emotions, and our perception of them, can contribute to our evaluation of her and her actions. Similarly, the examination of one's own emotions and feelings may sometimes be morally important and revelatory.

It is widely recognized that emotions in the capacity of states to which we are subject may distract, mislead or even incapacitate. The Stoics' therapeutic efforts were often focused on getting rid of emotions in this sense, for example, the fear of death. (*See*, STOIC ETHICS.) As examples such as fear show, emotions may have an object towards which they are directed. In this sense they may possess cognitive or intentional content, unlike moods such as anxiety. Notably, although the object of an emotion might sometimes be also neutrally available to the subject without the colouring of the emotion, the emotive mode itself of experiencing the object isn't anything neutrally available. For example, while an object of fear may be neutrally available to the agent after she has realized that there was nothing to fear, the quality of the object's fearfulness itself is only available through the emotive response or reaction. (The emotion may, of course, be described for the purposes of communication). This suggests a more positive role for emotions as part of moral cognition. Sometimes our emotive responses may also be moral responses, and insofar as this is correct, there are moral responses or perceptions that by their very nature assume the form of emotive responses or experiences.

For instance, in the case of an experience of something as contemptible or disgusting we apparently can't separate the moral response from the emotive response, and the quality of something being contemptible or disgusting isn't available to us in any other way except through an emotive response. (Again descriptions of such responses can serve the purpose of communicating our moral views. An example is 'He made me want to puke' which can function as an expression of moral disgust or contempt.) Remorse in the sense of a painful realization of the meaning and value of one's action may also be used to exemplify how moral value can sometimes be properly comprehended or be fully available only through an emotive response. In such cases moral comprehension assumes the form of an emotive response or reaction. Such responses and reactions, one might say, constitute modes of understanding moral value. For example, reading about torture with horror and disgust might be characterized as a form or mode of understanding what is at stake morally. Furthermore, perhaps the moral significance of certain emotions such as sympathy, love and compassion might be characterized by saying that in guiding our attention they enable us to fully understand what the morally salient features of a situation are. (In the case of love's moral significance more specifically, one doesn't need to assume that we should be able to feel love towards strangers, for example. But already seeing someone as a possible object of someone's love, as someone's son, brother, husband or father, may make a difference to how we perceive that person, as Raimond Gaita has pointed out.)

But, one might ask, aren't emotive responses subjective and doesn't the preceding suggestion about their positive cognitive role therefore amount to envisaging morality as something subjective? Insofar as it is possible (sometimes) to distinguish between correct and incorrect emotive responses, the question can be answered negatively. To experience something emotively, one might say, is to see it in a particular light or to experience it in a particular way. To experience it thus, however, can be correct or incorrect. A mistake or misconception might be involved, as in the case of a fearful reaction, when there was nothing to fear. Similarly, my feelings of loyalty or respect might disappear upon realizing the true character of the person or group towards whom I felt loyalty. More broadly, besides being correct or incorrect, an emotional response may also be appropriate or inappropriate. An example is one's reaction being out of proportion. In such a case the reaction might not be mistaken in the sense that there really was a reason to be angry, only no reason to be *so* angry. Thus, the distinctions between the correctness and incorrectness of emotive responses on the one hand, and between their appropriateness and inappropriateness on the other hand, aren't the same. But however exactly these two distinctions are related, in answering the question raised above it is important to observe that emotions can be influenced by reason or other considerations. This corrigibility of emotions distinguishes them from merely subjective responses and reactions.

More specifically, that an object may merit or deserve a certain emotive response (e.g. respect or loyalty) shows that there is a normative aspect to emotive reactions and responses, and that the distinction between correct and incorrect can indeed be applied to them. The applicability of considerations of merit or desert means that a subject's emotive reactions aren't simply to be seen as caused by their object, producing a certain reaction in the subject on the basis of her psychological makeup. This also means that a person can be held responsible for her emotions, at least to an extent. These interconnected points suggest that emotions shouldn't be contrasted with reason in the sense of being something non-rational or even irrational. Instead, the intellectual and affective dimensions of human existence apparently ought to be philosophical conceived of as more closely allied than philosophers have tended to do. (*See also,* LITERATURE'S ETHICAL SIGNIFICANCE, CARE.)

Further reading

Nussbaum, M. (2001), *Upheavals of Thought: The Intelligence of Emotions.* Cambridge: Cambridge University Press.
Oakley, J. (1993), *Morality and the Emotions*. London: Routledge.
Williams, B. (1973), 'Morality and the Emotions', in *Problems of the Self.* Cambridge: Cambridge University Press, pp. 207–229.

Evil

The term 'evil' seems distinctive in the sense that, in contrast to the other two abstract negative moral terms, 'bad' and 'wrong', its use appears to be primarily moral. Whereas bad or wrong isn't always morally bad or wrong, evil apparently is. In the past, especially in connection with the theological so-called problem of evil (see below), philosophers talked of catastrophic natural events, such as earthquakes, as natural evils. This, however, seems to assume an apparently problematic conception of an intelligent being, a God (or gods), who is responsible for natural evils. Insofar as talk about natural evil expresses a desire to morally criticize the agent behind evil natural events, such talk is to be seen as a special case of the moral employment of 'evil'. Otherwise, natural evils don't seem to have any moral relevance. (Jean-Jacques Rousseau (1712–1778) was the first to emphasize the need to treat natural and moral evil differently.) But is evil something different from morally bad? What is evil and how should evil actions be explained?

Often philosophers don't distinguish between the morally bad and evil. For example, neither Socrates nor Kant makes any such distinction, but both seem to regard anything morally bad as evil. One of the few philosophers to distinguish between the concepts of bad and evil as the opposites of good is Friedrich Nietzsche. (See, NIETZSCHE.) As regards everyday language and thinking, to describe something as evil seems the most severe condemnation available. Not just anything morally bad is evil, but only exceptionally bad acts like murder and the torture of innocents. A prime example of evil is the Holocaust and the systematic destruction of human lives it involved. However, whether the characterization of evil as something 'exceptionally bad' implies that the difference between evil and moral bad is merely quantitative isn't clear. Consequently, it also remains unclear how the relation between the concepts of bad and evil is to be characterized. Partly adding to the difficulties is that philosophers have had relatively little to say about evil as distinct from moral bad. Rather than anything carefully clarified, the concept of evil seems to be given up to rhetorical uses, for example, by politicians. But thus employed it can shed little light on the nature of relevant actions. Rather, it is presumably part of the purpose of the 'rhetoric of evil' to silence attempts to comprehend the nature of so-called evil actions.

One might seek to characterize the difference between bad and evil by saying that, whereas bad may be something unintended (an accidental consequence or a by-product of something), evil is always intended. Doing evil is doing something bad for its own sake; it is the pursuit of suffering and destruction for the sake of suffering and destruction. Hence, in the case of evil, not only the consequences but also the intentions of the agent are evil. (Sometimes evil in this sense is called 'pure' or 'absolute' and contrasted with mixed forms that combine evil outcomes with good or neutral intentions.) But although this characterization may bring to view something about evil, there are cases it doesn't capture. As Hannah Arendt observes, not all evil seems demonic in the sense of involving evil intentions. Rather than manifesting wicked and malicious intentions, and perhaps exhibiting dark 'satanic greatness', this kind of evil is banal and mundane. Here the perpetrators' personal motives, if any are discernible, are merely petty, for example, relating to career advancement. This is exemplified by Adolf Eichmann who was responsible for organizing the transportation of the victims of the Nazis to the death-camps, and on whose trial Arendt famously reported. Notably, his motives such as career advancement have no essential connection with the evil he committed, but they could have been satisfied in a number of ways besides mass-murder. Consequently, Eichmann's motives don't seem evil in themselves or as such, though the evil of what he did can't be denied.

This brings to view the problem posed by evil and evil actions: their apparent incomprehensibility. Evil actions don't seem to spring from any readily understandable motives, such as desire for personal gain, that could account for the actions in proportion to their badness. In this sense they defy explanation. This holds especially for evil in the sense discussed by Arendt. For, even if one might be tempted to to explain away evil actions based on evil intentions by saying that such actions ultimately serve the selfish satisfaction of perverse desires, or perhaps are expressions of mental disturbances (as serial killers are often characterized), this explanation isn't satisfactory for the type of cases Arendt discusses. Eichmann wasn't mentally disturbed and apparently didn't get any perverted satisfaction from his actions. Nor did he get any personal gains proportional to the gravity of his deeds. And as Arendt also explains, Eichmann didn't have any particularly strong ideological convictions, for example, strong anti-Semitic feelings.

This function of the concept of evil as marking a limit of comprehensibility comes to view also in connection with the theological problem of evil.

Here the problem is to explain the existence of evil in the world, assuming that an omnipotent and benevolent God has created the world. On this background, evil seems anomalous and requires explanation. (See God AND RELIGION.) Similarly, in the case of evil actions an explanation not otherwise required for actions appears to be needed. Problematically, however, this circumstance of perplexity can also be easily exploited in support of rhetorical uses of 'evil'. A temptation arises here to explain evil actions by reference to a mysterious force of evil at work in the people perceived as enemies. Moreover, it isn't clear that explanations by reference to perversions and mental disturbances manage to do much more than remove evil from the normal order of things. 'Disturbance' and 'perversion', after all, only mark deviation.

How is evil to be explained? There are only a few philosophical attempts to do so. Kant discusses this problem in his *Religion within the Boundaries of Mere Reason,* where he presents his famous thesis about the radically evil nature of the human. According to Kant, in order for a person to be held morally responsible for an action, she must have freely chosen to act in that way. This means that, for instance, the Biblical account of original sin as the source of evil must be rejected as incompatible with morality. For, if something in history caused the evil actions of humans, then we couldn't be held responsible for them. (See, FREEDOM.) Rather, Kant argues, at the very root of human capacity for choice lies a propensity to evil.

This propensity to evil is connected with the sensible nature of humans, although sensibility as such doesn't make anyone act immorally. We can always, in principle, will to act according to the moral law. (See, KANT and GROUNDWORK.) Nevertheless, often enough our actions are motivated by the impulses of sensibility or selfishness (self-love) rather than the moral law. According to Kant, this human propensity to evil has three forms: (1) The weakness of heart or our frailty in living up to moral values: we know what's right but act otherwise; (2) the impurity of heart: our will combines pure moral and impure incentives, and can act on mixed motives; for example, sometimes we believe we are acting out of respect for the moral law but are really acting selfishly; (3) the wickedness, corruption or perversity of heart: given our freedom we have the capacity to choose maxims other than moral ones and to subordinate the incentives of the moral law to such non-moral maxims. Thus, we can systematically substitute non-moral maxims for moral ones, and in this sense have a capacity for evil. By 'radical evil' Kant refers to this human propensity to choose immorally. Although this propensity is universal in humans, as rational beings they can't renounce the moral law altogether. Even when they don't obey the moral law, they still recognize its authority. Indeed, it is an essential part of Kant's account that evil action requires comprehending the good but choosing against it. (For the notion of a maxim, *see GROUNDWORK*.)

Alternatively, one might try to explain the evil actions of individuals in terms of the Socratic account of evil as something done out of ignorance. In stark opposition to Kant, this explanation denies the possibility of choosing evil knowingly. As Socrates argues, doing evil would be a matter of choosing the worse thing for the better, and only a fool would do that. When we do evil, we *think* it is something is good, although it isn't. (*See*, SOCRATES.) In the light of this account, the evil actions of particular individuals might then be explained as based on ignorance regarding some specific matters. Although the agent believes her actions will result in something good for her (e.g. that murdering someone will satisfy her desire for revenge, give peace of mind and relieve her suffering), she is mistaken. If the person understood the situation, her own attitudes and reactions better, she wouldn't choose to do those things. From this point of view, to oppose evil we must then gain knowledge, in particular self-knowledge. Evil can be countered only by coming to better understand ourselves and the world. Recently, a Socratic account of this type has been developed by Daryl Koehn.

Another, not unrelated, way of thinking about evil is Arendt's account of the banality of evil. Here evil done can't be traced back to the agent's particular wickedness, pathology, ideological conviction, selfishness, and so on, but as Arendt remarks about Eichmann, his '[. . .] only personal distinction was a perhaps extraordinary shallowness' (Arendt 1964, 159). Accordingly, it is by reference to this shallowness that Arendt explains the evil committed by Eichmann. The explanation for his actions is his thoughtlessness or inability to think. Eichmann never properly realized what he was doing. And this is what, according to Arendt, the greatest evil-doers are like. They never gave a proper thought to the matter. Crucially, this absence of thinking means that for them there is no consideration or judgment to hold them back.

Hence, Arendt maintains, not unlike Socrates, that it is thinking that can prevent us from falling into evil. Notably, however, lack of thinking isn't the same as lack of knowledge. Although people can't be required to know, because it isn't anything they can do at will, they can in a certain sense be required to think, irrespective of the level of their ignorance or intelligence. Or as Arendt also explains, imagination (similarly subject to willing) is crucial because it enables us to see things in proper perspective. According to her, philosophy, in the capacity of the exercise of the faculty of thought, is also needed to prevent evil, although there's a possibility that it will arrive on the scene too late. She writes, commenting of the Socratic idea that we only do evil out of ignorance: 'The most conspicuous and most dangerous fallacy in the proposition as old as Plato, "Nobody does evil voluntarily," is the implied conclusion, "Everyone wants to do good." The sad truth of the matter is that most evil is done by people who never made up their mind to be either bad or good.' (Arendt 2003, 181) Importantly, this behaviour of never making up their minds to be good or bad doesn't merely have to do with the psychology of individuals. It is also encouraged by certain kinds of political systems, such as totalitarianism, which requires a certain lack of spontaneity, for example, to think for oneself, from its subjects. It is this lack of spontaneity that Arendt detected in Eichmann. And of course there may also be other forms of political organization, besides totalitarianism, that promote this kind of lack of spontaneity.

Further reading

Arendt, H. (2003), 'Thinking and Moral Considerations', in J. Kohn (ed.), *Responsibility and Judgment*. New York: Schocken Books.

Arendt, H. (2006), *Eichmann in Jerusalem: A Report on the Banality of Evil*. London: Penguin Books.

Bernstein, R. J. (2002), *Radical Evil: A Philosophical Interrogation*. Cambridge: Polity.

Koehn, D. (2005), *The Nature of Evil*. New York: Palgrave.

Freedom

Freedom, and the concept thereof, is important for morality and moral philosophy in a number of ways. Accordingly, questions about freedom have been raised and approached by philosophers from a variety of different angles. To begin with, freedom is a precondition for holding an agent morally responsible and, therefore, a condition of moral praise, blame, and so on. However, this can be understood in more than one way. First, as a condition of moral responsibility, freedom may be regarded a condition of the possibility of morality overall – a point which Kant emphasizes. (*See*, KANT and GROUND-WORK.) Conceived as such a general condition, the problem whether humans are free emerges as an abstract question about the freedom of the will, that is, whether humans are in principle capable of free choice and action. The practical relevance of this theoretical problem isn't clear however. If someone proved that free will doesn't exist, would a rational response be to abandon morality and any moral considerations?

Secondly, even if we assume that humans are free in principle, the question remains whether particular individuals or actions are actually free. How this second question is answered in a particular case is relevant, again, for whether the agent can be held morally responsible. The answer to this question, however, no longer affects the more abstract issue of the possibility of morality overall and freedom of the will. That question isn't about the actuality of anyone's freedom in particular but the actuality of freedom presupposes its possibility in principle. (Note also that responsibility should be understood here more broadly than as merely responsibility for *actions*. An agent might also be held responsible for being in a state of drunkenness or drug addiction, and consequently for actions in these states, even if drug addiction may be a state of unfreedom in a certain sense.) The second question about the actuality of freedom also gives rise to further questions about what freedom is or requires and how to achieve it. The practical relevance of these questions is more direct than that of the question about the freedom of the will. The latter questions also have connections with political questions about freedom. Generally speaking, the problem of what freedom is and how it can be achieved, can be approached from two alternate angles: as concerning external constraints on freedom, as in the case of political control, or as concerning internal constraints on freedom, as in our restricting our own freedom. This distinction isn't always clear-cut.

A broader abstract sense in which freedom might be considered a condition of morality overall is the following. Freedom in the sense of a capacity to choose to bring about certain states of affairs or to produce outcomes – rather than their just occurring or coming into existence on their own – seems a condition of rational agency and the possibility of action. Insofar as freedom is a precondition of moral agency in this sense, its relevance for morality and moral philosophy extends well beyond issues of moral responsibility. In this latter sense freedom is also a condition of the possibility of any of the projects of moral development or perfection that an agent might undertake.

A highly influential discussion of freedom is Mill's *On Liberty*, concerned mainly with the limits of society's legitimate power over the individual. But the issue isn't merely political liberty, Mill emphasizes. There are forms of 'social tyranny' that go deeper than political tyranny, in that they leave fewer means of escape, 'enslaving the soul itself'. (*OL*, 9) Protection is therefore needed against domination by prevailing opinions and feelings, and against the tendency of society to impose its ideas and practices upon its members, thus preventing the formation of individuality that doesn't conform to their dictates.

As a way to define the limit of society's power over the individual, Mill suggests the liberalist principle that the only warrant for interfering with an individual's freedom is self-protection or preventing harm to others. An individual's presumed own good, by contrast, doesn't suffice to justify interference. Thus, according to Mill, the appropriate region of human freedom is whatever affects solely the individual herself and others by consent. This includes liberty of thought and expression, including publication, and the 'liberty of tastes and pursuits; of framing the plan of our life to suit our own character; of doing as we like' as long as others are not harmed 'even though they should think our conduct foolish, perverse or wrong.' (*OL*, 17) Without this freedom to pursue one's own GOOD in one's own way, a society, according to Mill, can't be characterized as free.

Mill presents a threefold argument for the freedom of thought and expression, from which he concludes that neither the government nor the common opinion has the right to control the expression of opinion. First, to deny freedom to express views that differ from the received ones assumes the infallibility of those who hold the received view. But since humans aren't infallible, in order to avoid error and to arrive at truth, freedom of opinion must be accepted. Secondly, even if the divergent views were wrong, they might still contain a partial truth, and thus help to correct the received view, wherever it falls short the whole truth. Thirdly, even assuming the truth of the received view, unless the grounds for and against it are understood, the received view doesn't count as knowledge. When simply accepted without understanding its grounds, a view is entertained as mere prejudice and superstition. Thus, as Mill famously states: 'If all mankind minus one, were of one opinion, and only one person were of the contrary opinion, mankind would be no more justified in silencing that one person, than he, if he had the power, would be justified in silencing mankind.' (OL, 21)

Actions on the other hand, because of how they may affect others, shouldn't be given the same freedom as expression of opinion, Mill holds. Indeed, in certain circumstances the expression of an opinion, whose publication in the press should be allowed, may constitute an unacceptable act; for example, when the purpose is to incite a mob to violence. Again, the limit of the authority of the society over individuals is that their behaviour should not injure others. But when an individual only hurts herself, this is an inconvenience society should bear 'for the sake of greater good of human freedom'. (OL, 91) Nevertheless, Mill rejects the objection that his view is a form of selfish indifference according to which humans have nothing to do with each other's conduct of life.

Ultimately, Mill's argument for freedom and individuality is based on considerations of utility. (See, UTILITARIANISM and CONSEQUENTIALISM.) Self-development and the development of individual character makes a human being not only more valuable to herself, but also to others. This is why society should let strong and exceptional individuals develop, and allow its members to lead different lives. More specifically, individuality and diversity are important, in Mill's view, because uniformity and conformism lead to stagnation and in this way work against creativity and progress. On the other hand, given that people's sources of pleasure are different and their susceptibility to pain differs, happiness in this sense too requires allowing diversity in modes of life.

A notable characteristic of Mill's discussion of freedom is his focus on its external, social and political constraints. But what about the ways in which we may ourselves constrain our freedom, and prevent ourselves from realizing it? For example, we may restrict our freedom through our preconceptions regarding either particular issues or how to live life in general, and in this way prevent ourselves from doing certain things or pursuing certain paths of life. Such constraints may often originate in the society, and are merely internalized by us. In this regard they might be understood as forms of society's 'enslavement of our souls' in Mill's phrase. However, when it comes to the task of releasing ourselves from such constraints, any principles, such as Mill seeks to establish, whose purpose is to regulate the authority of the society over us, seem of little help and relevance. Rather, we ourselves must work on ourselves, for example, releasing ourselves from our preconceptions and other problematic attitudes, in order to achieve freedom. Indeed, here it would seem problematic to assume that individuals are, so to speak, born free, and only subsequently enslaved by the society. If our identities and individualities are partly social constructs, and our modes of being and acting adopted partly from the environment, then perhaps there is no starting point where we truly are free. (Infants, when they can't yet act, aren't free; but when they have reached that point, perhaps they are no longer free.) If so, freedom is really an achievement, not a birthright (to use Daryl Koehn's phrase).

The problem of what freedom is and how it can be achieved has been discussed from this angle by, for example, the Stoic philosopher Epictetus. Indeed, while Epictetus – a former slave himself – recognizes that there are external constraints on freedom, he maintains that the power they exert over us depends ultimately on us. For example, one can only be threatened by what one fears or wants to avoid, and these are attitudes that the agent herself takes towards particular things. But if the power of external things over us depends on us, then only we ourselves can liberate ourselves. No one, including society, can bestow on us our freedom.

Part of Epictetus' (or more broadly the Stoics') conception is that a central component of our unfreedom is our mistaken conceptions of things, and the resultant misdirection of our desires in the wrong objects. We enslave ourselves through our misconceptions, and by desiring things that are not under our control. For instance, we fear things that need not be feared, and consequently restrict our actions in unnecessary ways. (*See*, STOIC ETHICS.) According to Epictetus, 'That man is free who lives as he wishes; who can neither be compelled, nor hindered nor constrained; whose impulses are unimpeded, who attains his desires and doesn't fall into what he wants to avoid.' (*Discourses*, 227) The key to freedom, in this view, is a correct understanding of the nature of things. In Epictetus' metaphor, just as knowledge of how to play the harp prevents one from being hindered and restrained in one's playing, so knowledge of how to live enables one to live unhindered and unrestrained. But emancipation for Epictetus isn't merely an intellectual enterprise. It requires also training our other attitudes.

The connection between (the concepts of) freedom, knowledge and truth that comes to view here is also illustrated by the fact that, when we are prevented from doing something that we mistakenly think we want to do, this isn't perceived as an infringement of our freedom. As Mill explains, stopping someone from going on a bridge which is about to collapse, when the person doesn't know this fact and doesn't want to fall into the river, isn't a real infringement of her liberty. For 'liberty consists in doing what one desires, and he does not desire to fall into the river.' (*OL*, 107) Accordingly, to avoid running against obstacles that prevent me from reaching my goals and thus restrict what I can do (and therefore my freedom), I need to know what I'm doing and to understand the nature of things, so to speak.

It would then seem narrow to conceive the problem of the freedom of thought and action as merely a problem about society preventing us from thinking, expressing our thoughts, and acting. Partly, and perhaps more significantly, the problem is that we ourselves may prevent ourselves from thinking and acting freely. For example, it might be the very modes of thinking that we have adopted (perhaps inherited from a tradition), and which seem entirely unquestionable to us, that prevent us from understanding something or doing something. In this sense and more generally, we might sometimes not even be properly aware of the obstacles to our freedom; the obstacles may be modes of being and thinking we have adopted unconsciously and quite unnoticed. However, insofar as philosophy is capable of drawing our attention to such things, and can help us find alternative ways of thinking and acting, it can be comprehended as a liberating and emancipatory practice, as Epictetus, among others, understands it. Thus conceived, philosophy is something we may take up and use to transform ourselves and to achieve freedom. More recently, these themes have been taken up by Michel Foucault.

Further reading

Epictetus (1995), 'On Freedom', in C. Gill (ed.), *The Discourses of Epictetus*. London: Everyman, pp. 227–245.

Mill, J. S. (1991), 'On Liberty', in J. Gray (ed.), *On Liberty and Other Essays*. Oxford: Oxford University Press, pp. 1–128.

Oksala, Johanna (2005), *Foucault on Freedom*. Cambridge: Cambridge University Press.

God and religion

Religious theories of morality regard God (or gods) as the foundation of morality. Roughly, what is GOOD and right, and how we should live, is taken to be determined by God, or in any case, to be communicated to us through God – however we might conceive of the justification of any interpretations of God's will. (See, DEONTOLOGICAL ETHICS.)

Although ancient Greek ethical thinking is generally secular, and medieval moral philosophy is quite directly influenced by ancient philosophy, Christian religious ideas play an important role in medieval philosophy. An example is Thomas Aquinas (1225–1274), an Aristotelian philosopher and theologian. His ethics is a version of Aristotelian VIRTUE ETHICS with Christian modifications. Like Aristotle, he takes the task of moral philosophy to be twofold: to determine the ultimate goal of human existence and to determine how this goal can be achieved. Following Aristotle, Aquinas identifies the goal of human life as happiness, but reinterprets it as a life according, not only to reason, but God. For Aquinas, virtues form the foundation of ethics, virtue concepts constituting the centre of his theory. But while his list of virtues has significant overlap with Aristotle's, it also includes additional so-called theological virtues: faith, hope and charity not recognized by the Greeks. Similarly, not all the Greek virtues of a noble man fit the Christian list (See, ARISTOTLE AND NICOMACHEAN ETHICS.).

Christian religious ideas don't only play an important role in medieval philosophy when it comes to issues of morality. Philosophers in this period make use of the notion of God in other areas too, often when trying to explain whatever seems otherwise difficult to explain. This trend continues to the early-modern period, with one example being how Descartes (1596–1650) makes use of the idea of the benevolence of God in response to the problem of scepticism. Ultimately, according to him, our knowledge of the external world is guaranteed by God not wishing to deceive us. Closer to moral philosophy, Leibniz's (1646–1716) answer to the problem of EVIL, that is, why there is evil in the world, relies on the theological/metaphysical idea of God as a perfect, benevolent being. Because God as a perfect being would not choose the actual world to be nothing less than best overall, the actual world is the best possible of all possible worlds. (See also, EVIL.) Kant, in turn, can be characterized as a modern, secular thinker in the sense that God plays no role in his theoretical philosophy. For Kant the enlightenment ideal that we should think for ourselves rather than be guided by some religious or other authority is central, and marks a difference between his and earlier thinking.

Nevertheless, God enters Kant's moral philosophy 'through the backdoor', so to speak. For the most part he makes no use of the concept of God in the development of his ethics. Indeed, for Kant, any attempt to base the moral law on God's commands would be heteronomous, that is, contradictory to the idea of the autonomy of the moral agent. (*See*, KANT.) However, Kant is ultimately forced to appeal to the idea of God and the immortality of the soul to deal with the unwanted outcome of his thought that living according to the laws of morality might constitute an unhappy life. That is, he is led to appeal to God in order to re-establish a connection between the concepts of moral worth and happiness, which he separates in the earlier phases of his argument. As Kant explains, the highest GOOD (in the sense of complete good) consists in the union of moral action and personal happiness. This can only be approached by human beings, and its perfection, becoming worthy of happiness, requires an infinite time. This seems to make it necessary to assume God and the immortality of soul as postulates of practical reason. (Such postulates don't extend our theoretical knowledge and, Kant argues, there can be no knowledge of God. But, from a practical point of view, we are nevertheless entitled to such postulates, insofar as the possibility of morality requires them.) Ultimately, God serves to harmonize the laws of nature and morality so as to guarantee the union of moral action and happiness.

Kant's appeal to God therefore still resembles earlier philosophers' use of God to explain whatever their theories can't explain. Perhaps for this reason it typically goes unmentioned by contemporary Kantians. On the basis of Kant's philosophy Schopenhauer develops an ethics entirely without God, diverging from Kant by making sympathy towards living beings the central notion of his ethics. Thus, for Schopenhauer, there is no need or room to appeal to God. Other philosophical critics of religion, who in their ways contribute to the secularization of European culture in the spirit of enlightenment, include Hume, Karl Marx (1818–1883) and Nietzsche. (*See* HUME, NIETZSCHE.) A particular focus of Hume's criticism is the irrationality of religious rules: by contrast to the rules of JUSTICE, the superstitious rules of religion don't benefit us, and are in this sense against reason. Marx and Nietzsche emphasize the function of religion as an instrument of power and oppression.

According to Marx, religion is a source of illusory happiness that must be abolished along the way to real happiness. It is both a source of and a remedy to suffering, in his famous phrase, 'opium of the people'. Similarly, Nietzsche regards Christianity as a comforting illusion that has helped the oppressed to bear their suffering. Equally famously, Nietzsche declares God dead now that the illusion has been revealed as what it is. On the other hand, as he also notes, if we simply substitute atheism, reason and science in the place of Christianity, and let it take a position of the monopoly to truth, nothing much has changed. (*See*, NIETZSCHE.) Among contemporary philosophers, whose thinking generally tends to be secular, a notable exception is Levinas in whose work religion is an important theme. (*See*, LEVINAS.)

Good

Good is one of the central moral concepts, sometimes treated as *the* central concept by reference to which others are to be explained. Its centrality doesn't make it any easier to explain, however. Rather than implying simplicity, the centrality and importance of the concept seem indicative of its manifoldness or multiplicity. By contrast to normative or deontological concepts such as right and OBLIGATION, good may be characterized as a value term. (*See*, OBLIGATION.) Good has two main contrasts: bad and EVIL. The so-called value-theory is a study of the nature of goodness and what things are good.

As this characterization of value-theory indicates, the word 'good' is ambiguous in the sense that it is used, in one instance, to talk about the goodness of something and, in another, to talk about good things or goods, that is, the bearers of goodness, so to speak. Accordingly, the ambiguous question 'what is good?' might be responded to by listing good things, but also by trying to explain what goodness is. (*See*, PRINCIPIA ETHICA.) By the concept of good we might understand the complex whole exhibited by the uses of the word 'good' in the sense of goodness. For, even after taking into account its ambiguity, the concept can still be applied to a variety of different kinds of cases. To characterize something as good (as possessing goodness) seems to mean something different in the case of, for example, good weather, knife or a person. If so, one may say that there are many different forms of goodness; the concept doesn't seem to possess any simple unity that could be stated in an overarching definition. (That as such, however, doesn't mean the concept is ambiguous, and is not to be seen as indicative of its ambiguity.) Only some of the uses of the concept are moral, as the examples just given show; the concept also has a multitude of non-moral uses. While it seems very difficult to explain what is distinctive to the uses of the concept of good in a moral sense, we might say very roughly that moral concepts are generally applicable to humans and their actions only, including their characters, motives, and the outcomes of their actions. Sometimes moral concepts may be extensible to animals, for example, heroic dogs, but they don't seem applicable to inanimate objects, processes, and so on. (*See also*, EVIL.)

It is not self-evident that good, even in its moral sense, constitutes a unitary concept. Nietzsche, for example, argues that 'good', when contrasted alternatively with 'bad' or 'evil', means different things. These different meanings of 'good', according to him, belong to two different systems of morality, of which the present European morality is a descendant. (*See*, NIETZSCHE.) G. H. von Wright presents a different analysis of the concept in *The Varieties of Goodness*, distinguishing many different forms of goodness. His attitude isn't really typical among philosophers, however. By contrast to von Wright's willingness to recognize many different forms of goodness, also in the case of the moral employments of the concept, philosophers often display a tendency to try to explain the concept of moral good in terms of some specific use of 'good', perceived as fundamental. An example is Mill's attempt to reduce moral goodness to hedonic good and to identify goodness with pleasure. (*See*, UTILITARIANISM. Another prominent representative of hedonism is Epicurus.) A different view is taken by Moore, according to whom the concept of good isn't definable either in natural or metaphysical terms. (*See*, PRINCIPIA ETHICA, THICK AND THIN MORAL CONCEPTS.)

If one accepts the manifoldness of the concept of good, one might then say (as Wittgenstein does) that each different kind of use of the word 'good' constitutes a facet of the concept which, overall, is a conglomerate of these different uses. (For reasons discussed by von Wright, however, the concept is presumably not appropriately characterized as a so-called family-resemblance concept.) Apparently common to all uses of the concept of good is that whatever is good is desirable, or preferable to what isn't good or less good. To simply say that good is something desirable, however, seems hardly a satisfactory characterization of the concept. This merely illustrates its abstractness and lack of specific descriptive content. (There are apparent exceptions to the characterization of good as something desirable. One might, for instance, describe someone as a good boy or a good girl, meaning something like proper, obedient, and unadventurous and therefore boring. Thus, one might prefer the more interesting company of bad boys and girls, and even regard them as morally better in the sense of being less inclined to conformism. But this case presumably is a derivative one, expressing opposition to goodness in the sense of Christian virtuousness and dutifulness, here perceived as something undesirable. Thus, the matter seems to boil down to a dispute about whether something often called 'good' really is good.)

Of particular interest to moral philosophers has been the notion of intrinsic good or goodness as something good in itself or good as such, not good for the sake of anything else. A traditional example of something that is intrinsically good is happiness which we seem to want simply for its own sake, not for the sake of anything further. (*See*, Aristotle.) Kant maintains that the only thing good in itself or good unconditionally is the good will; anything else can amount to or result in something bad or evil. (*See*, *groundwork*.) Intrinsic good then appears fundamental to our valuations in the sense that the value of other things appears to ultimately depend on what is intrinsically good. Accordingly, intrinsic good seems to constitute an ultimate or final end of our actions, that for the sake of which anything else is pursued. Sometimes the term 'highest good' (*summum bonum*) is used for intrinsic good. Value monists hold that there is solely one kind of intrinsic good, while pluralists maintain there are many different kinds. Some philosophers reject the notion of an intrinsic good, maintaining that everything good is good relatively. There are also certain ambiguities relating to the concept of intrinsic good that I have left out of discussion. (For a discussion of the latter, see Korsgaard's article below.)

A category of things whose goodness depends on something further, and that are not intrinsically good, is instrumental goodness. The goodness of instrumentally good depends on the value of whatever it is good for, in the capacity of a means to that further good. Instrumental goods however don't exhaust the class of non-intrinsic goods, contrary to what is sometimes assumed. For the goodness of something may also depend on the goodness of something else in a different sense. For example, to have a negative HIV-test result may be good, but its goodness is neither intrinsic nor (typically) instrumental. That it is a means to intrinsic good therefore isn't the only way in which a non-intrinsically good thing can derive its value from what is intrinsically good.

Modern moral philosophers are divided on the issue of whether the concept of good or the concept of right is more fundamental. With respect to this, utilitarians have held that goodness explains what is morally right, while Kantians have held the opposite view and explained good by reference to what is right. (For the concept of right and further discussion of this issue, see Obligation.)

Further reading

Korsgaard, C. M. (1983), 'Two Distinctions in Goodness', *The Philosophical Review*, 92, (2), 196–195.
von Wright, G. H. (1963), *The Varieties of Goodness*. London: Routledge.

Impartiality

Impartiality is often regarded as central to morality. Sometimes it is even taken to be a necessary constituent of morality, or still more strongly, morality is identified with the adoption of an impartial attitude. The requirement of impartiality means that no one's personal values, needs, interests or desires ought, as such, to be privileged over those of others. Rather, everyone's interests and needs should be given equal weight. Hence, from an impartial, neutral point of view, each agent counts as equivalent; no one has intrinsically more significance than anyone else. For example, I ought to demand the same from me as from others (or not less from myself anyway), and I shouldn't use double standards that benefit me or those close to me. Instead, my personal point of view is to be treated as one among many. But although impartiality in this sense certainly seems part of morality, philosophers continue to debate on how exactly it is to be understood and construed as a constituent of morality. Impartiality, in the sense of the adoption of the impersonal point of view of an ideal observer detached from all interests and points of view, has been argued to be a mere fiction by Iris Marion Young. But even if this is correct, it may still leave open alternate ways in which to construe the notion.

Impartiality is sometimes assumed to follow from the requirement of UNIVERSAL-IZABILITY of moral judgments, but this seems incorrect. It would be perfectly compatible with the requirement of UNIVERSALIZABILITY to run the world according to, for instance, my preferences, as long as we would consistently stick to the principles that express those preferences. Thus, impartiality involves more than mere universality. It requires taking into account the interests and positions of others. (*See*, UNIVERSALIZABILITY.)

Both Kantian and utilitarian ethics regard impartiality as essential to morality. In Kant's case, impartiality is, so to speak, built into the very notion of moral agency. A Kantian moral agent is a rational being who acts on the commands of reason. Those commands, however, are exactly the same for all rational beings and demand that we treat all rational beings alike. Morality, in this sense, abstracts from all contingent features of the agent, such as race or sex, relations to particular others, and personal preferences, and makes us all equal before morality. Thus, from Kant's perspective, impartiality emerges as an integral part of the constitution of morality. To adopt the point of view of morality is to adopt an impartial perspective. (*See*, KANT and *GROUNDWORK*) Utilitarianism, on the other hand, regards as the goal of morality the greatest happiness or welfare for the greatest number. Achieving this goal requires abstraction from the desires, interests, and so on, of any particular agents, and treating their desires and interests as no more important than anyone else's. In this sense the utilitarian conception of morality too requires the adoption of an impartial attitude. (*See*, CONSEQUENTIALISM, *UTILITARIANISM*.)

By contrast, impartiality isn't a similarly crucial component of, for instance, Aristotelian VIRTUE ETHICS, which regards morality as a motley of virtues, including partial ones such as friendship. (*See*, ARISTOTLE and *NICOMACHEAN ETHICS*.) Aristotle, however, fails to explain what is distinctive about acceptable forms of partiality, and consequently one might wonder whether his apparent acceptance of slavery and the inequality of women might be indicative of an unquestioned acceptance of partiality.

One might distinguish between strict and moderate impartialism. (Partialism too may come in more or less strong forms. Aristotle represents a moderate form.) Whereas strict impartialism requires one to be always impartial, the latter admits that impartiality doesn't always apply, and that it isn't a requirement for an action to count as moral. For example, one might not be required to treat one's own children just like any other children – which seems unloving and potentially cruel. More broadly, loyalty to one's family, friends or country might, in the right amount and situations, be seen as something morally worthy. Indeed, given that such special relationships as those with family and friends seem a key component of a happy life, one might ask whether a strictly impartial life, if it requires us to ignore such relationships, would be worth living at all? Whether there are forms of morally acceptable or even admirable partiality distinguishes partialists and moderate impartialists from strict impartialists.

According to some accounts, the utilitarian agent ought to be strictly impartial. On the other hand, utilitarians sometimes argue that practices such as giving special regard to one's own children or friendships are acceptable on the grounds that overall they contribute to the greatest happiness or welfare. In this way certain amounts of partiality can be built in into the utilitarian conception, as long as partiality is universally allowed for all agents in appropriate situations. Similarly, person-centred deontologism can make room for partiality by making duties person-relative. (*See*, DEONTOLOGICAL ETHICS.)

Nevertheless, it isn't entirely clear that these proposals can satisfactorily explain cases where partiality is acceptable or even admirable. Let's turn to problems that arise in connection with the requirement of impartiality.

As critics have argued, making impartiality part of morality in the manner of Kantian and utilitarian ethics leads to serious problems. First, strict impartiality seems too demanding. If everyone's needs, interests, and so on, must be given equal weight, then rather than being allowed to devote myself to my own projects, I would have an OBLIGATION to contribute equally to everyone else's, or indeed, if they were more urgent than mine, to devote all my efforts to them. Hence, assumed as a general principle that should guide all my actions, impartiality leads to an extremely demanding account of morality. The problem here, however, isn't merely that this would be impracticable and, presumably, lead to the agent's premature death, because she would be left with no time to relax or sleep. Secondly, part of being a person, and having a sense of identity and integrity, is having one's own projects, desires, plans, and so on, which have a special status for one because they are one's own. The point has been put by Bernard Williams as a criticism of utilitarianism: Only at the expense of personal integrity can one live one's life according to utilitarian morality, simply acting according to the calculations of overall good, whatever they may happen to be in the situations in which one finds oneself. Thirdly, strict impartiality would make it immoral to pay special attention to the needs of those close to one, for example, one's family or friends. For instance, one ought not to attend to one's own children or partner any more than to those of others. Besides the problems with this already mentioned, if impartiality forbade one from giving priority to any particular people, it would in this way threaten one's identity too, insofar as our personal identities are partly constituted through our special relationship to family, friends, home country, and so on. Strict impartiality would apparently undermine all this.

Now, what about the utilitarian moderate impartialist response that certain cases of partiality (such as everyone giving precedence to their own children) can be separately justified by reference to their contribution to happiness or welfare overall? It isn't clear that this is satisfactory. Imagine that I'm, on the mentioned grounds, allowed to be partial to the benefit of my partner, and save her from flames while leaving someone else to die. But if I act in this way because of the action's contribution to general happiness, rather than because she's my partner, I might be said to have 'one thought too many', in Williams' famous phrase (Williams 1981, 18). My partner would be rightly upset, if I told her that I did it for general happiness, not for her. And this objection seems to hold even if this 'one thought too many' is merely an afterthought – the justification of my instinctive action given afterwards, rather than the action's actual motive.

Here it seems helpful to ask, when is partiality or favouritism really morally problematic? Typically this seems to be the case whenever a person occupies a position or role connected with specific responsibilities and concerns. Examples are a judge or a state official or someone distributing a public resource, such as food aid. But favouritism seems problematic in such cases precisely because to take care of their tasks as they should, such people ought to act impartially. And that certainly doesn't imply that everyone should therefore be impartial all the time. Accordingly, perhaps neither partiality nor impartiality should be assumed as the dominant attitude inherently connected with morality, and built-in into an overarching philosophical account of morality from the start, as in Kantian and utilitarian ethics. Attempting to justify exceptions to the dominant attitude, we may well be arriving too late on the scene, unable to fix the problems, as difficulties with the utilitarian responses indicate. Instead, partiality and impartiality should perhaps be seen as connected with specific roles we occupy in life and society, whereby we also need to be alert to the fact that one may simultaneously occupy many such roles that should not be confused, as exemplified by a teacher who has her own child in the class.

Whether the explanation of the permissibility of partiality or obligatoriness of impartiality by reference to the agent's role must be understood in terms of person-centred deontology (which attributes different obligations and RIGHTS to different persons) isn't clear. (See, DEONTOLOGICAL ETHICS.) This issue will be left open here. (See also, OBLIGATION and CARE.)

Further reading

Cottingham, J. (1983), 'Ethics and Impartiality'. *Philosophical Studies,* 43, 83–99.
Darwall, S. (1983), *Impartial Reason*. Ithaca, NY: Cornell University Press.

Williams, B. (1981), 'Persons, Character and Morality', in *Moral Luck*. Cambridge: Cambridge University Press.

Young, I. M. (1990), 'The Ideal of Impartiality and the Civic Public', in *Justice and the Politics of Difference*. Princeton: Princeton University Press.

Justice

The notion of justice is of great importance to ethics. Any account of morality that ignores it seems substantially incomplete. Nevertheless, this presumably shouldn't be taken to mean that considerations of justice exhaust all moral considerations. Modern moral philosophy has been criticized for over-emphasizing abstract notions such as justice that involve the organization of moral relations in terms of universal rules or principles and require taking up an impartial attitude. (*See*, CARE, IMPARTIALITY.) As modern moral philosophy has understood justice, the purpose of rules of justice is principally to regulate the interactions between people, and protect them and their property against each other. But whether such an account of justice really captures all of its relevant aspects isn't clear.

The application of the concept of justice is wide in the sense that, besides social institutions such as states, laws, policies and practices, it can also be applied to individuals, groups and their actions. Traditionally, philosophers have tended to assume that underlying this variety there is a single unified essence of justice, so that justice is the same thing, for instance, in the case of a just person and a just state. This assumption is made explicitly by Plato and also, for instance, by Mill who subjects different examples of justice and injustice to examination with the purpose of determining what is common to them and in order to show that all instances of justice be explained in terms of utility. (*See*, UTILITARIANISM.) One might, however, question the legitimacy of this assumption of common essence (see below and METHODOLOGY).

An early sustained treatment of justice is Plato's REPUBLIC, where Socrates is challenged to explain his view that it is better to suffer than to commit injustice which involves him in a lengthy discussion of the nature of justice. (*See*, REPUBLIC.) Justice is also discussed in Aristotle's NICOMACHEAN ETHICS (Book V). Like Plato, Aristotle accepts the Socratic conception of justice as a state of the agent that disposes her to do just actions and wish for what is just. Aristotle, however, also draws a distinction between distributive and retributive (or rectificatory) justice that has since become standard. Distributive justice concerns what is proportionate; it has to do with a person getting what they deserve or what is fair. Retributive justice, on the other hand, is corrective; it is about equalizing the harm suffered by someone. Recently, the focus of philosophers has been on social justice, that is, on questions relating to the just organization of society. An influential treatment of this issue is John Rawls' A THEORY OF JUSTICE. Aristotle's legacy seems visible here in that often, as exemplified by Rawls, the problem of social justice is understood as a problem of distributive justice. It is taken to concern the distribution of goods, whereby this includes also the distribution of abstract goods, such as RIGHTS, opportunities, and so on. (*See,* A THEORY OF JUSTICE.)

Interestingly, Aristotle also remarks about justice, in connection with his discussion of friendship in *Nicomachean Ethics,* that when people are friends they have no need for justice. Apparently, he means that friends have no need for justice in the sense of guarantees or rules of justice. Rather, whenever there is friendship there is justice too and therefore no need for procedures that ascertain or guarantee it. Thus, the highest form of justice, Aristotle says, seems a matter of friendship. This brings to view a particular aspect of justice that is eclipsed when the focus of the discussion is on the problem of fairness. As Gaita has argued, there is a more fundamental problem relating to justice that precedes discussions of justice as fairness of distribution. This is the demand for the recognition of the full humanity of the people in question which involves the recognition of their individuality and the ascription of a full-blown inner life to them. For, without the latter, they can't be understood as capable of suffering wrong or injustice in the full sense.

Following Simone Weil and Iris Murdoch, Gaita speaks about this issue in terms of love, but certainly the recognition of someone as human in a full sense seems necessary for friendship too. (See also, EMOTIONS.) On the other hand, it seems characteristic of injustices such as racism and the inequality of women that their victims are not really recognized as fully human with, for instance, women being condescended to as being incapable of important decisions. This problem of blindness to the full humanity of certain people seems crucial to justice in the sense that, unless this blindness is overcome, it isn't possible to even begin to address the issue of justice as fairness. For fairness of distribution can only become an issue when the full human status of those who are protesting against unfairness isn't disputed. On the other hand, part of injustice in the sense outlined seems to be that the perpetrator might not even realize that something is wrong with how she treats certain people, and she may remain ignorant of the problem to begin with. (It is not uncommon for a sexist man, for example, to be quite unaware of his sexism.) Accordingly, it might be that sometimes blindness to relevant problems, rather than failure to act on them, explains the persistence of an injustice.

Crucially, the problem of justice therefore isn't merely, so to speak, a technical problem about how to organize relations with others, the society, or perhaps how to set up a global world order. The problem goes deeper. It is also a problem about understanding something accurately or seeing things as they are. Notably, however, a failure of this type – to recognize the other as fully human and to heed to her plea for justice – isn't simply about willingness to listen to the other either. A person or a group may be able to express themselves, or understand themselves, only quite poorly. Hence, it seems an idealization – perhaps often a convenient one – to maintain that demands of justice (or those for RIGHTS) should always come in the form of well articulated claims. (*See*, RIGHTS.)

As the preceding points indicate, there seem to be quite different considerations relating to justice, as exhibited by justice interpreted as fair treatment and distribution and justice as the recognition of a person's full humanity. These considerations might be taken to pertain to two different aspects of the concept of justice, neither of which is explainable in terms of the other. But if this is correct, it seems to be grounds for rejecting the assumption made by Plato and Mill, among others, that justice has a single unified essence. (Somewhat exceptionally, Adam Smith maintained that the term 'justice' has many meanings.)

As regards the approach to the problem of social justice, represented by Rawls and many others, characteristic of which is a conception of the problem as one of distribution of goods, this view has been criticized on other grounds too. Young argues that, while distributive issues are important to a satisfactory conception of justice, social justice can't be reduced to distribution. In particular, it is mistaken, according to her, to treat abstract goods such as rights, duties and opportunities as objects of distribution. This is to assume that rights, and so on, are static things to be distributed among recipients with a stable identity, and implies a misleading social ontology. For societies don't simply distribute goods to individuals who are there anyway: goods also constitute individuals, their identities and capacities. Accordingly, rights or opportunities aren't merely objects of distribution in the sense that rights, crucially, need to be exercised and opportunities taken up by their recipients, and their distribution as such doesn't ensure that. Rather than merely possessors and consumers, the members of society are also doers and actors. Consequently, justice may require addressing issues about how to get people to participate in and conceive of an institution as their own. Social justice is also about participation in deliberation and decision making and requires discussion of notions such as oppression and domination. Moreover, injustices such as those connected with class, sex or race also have to do with issues relating to culture, which Young characterizes as including symbols, images, meanings and stories through which people express themselves and communicate. Again, however, it isn't clear how potential problems relating to culture can be dealt with merely by addressing the organization of the state and its institutions. Problems here include issues such as the representation of certain groups in the media and prejudices against groups that might be deeply rooted in the imagination and language of people.

Important related criticisms of Rawls' theory of justice have been presented by Amartya Sen. For example, Rawls assumes that we can, and ought to arrive at a unique set of principles of justice. Sen, however, argues (with Bernard Williams) that disagreement doesn't necessarily have to be overcome, but can be an important and constitutive feature of our relations to others. Accordingly, there can be several conceptions of justice that survive critical scrutiny, and no compulsion to eliminate all but one, contrary to what Rawls assumes. But if we can't expect to arrive at a unanimous choice of principles in Rawls' so-called original position (or even a unique ranking of conceptions of justice, which is his weaker hope), then his idea of justice is inadequate, argues Sen. There is no public conception of justice in Rawls' sense that could serve as the basis of social institutions in the proceeding steps of his theory. (*See*, A THEORY OF JUSTICE.)

Connected with this is a second criticism that spells out a new starting point for a theory of social justice. Rather than trying to arrive at an account of perfect justice or ideal institutions, as Rawls aspires to, a theory of justice, according to Sen, should address the questions of enhancing justice and removing injustice. According to him, only a theory of this kind can serve as a basis for addressing problems of injustice in practice. This, however, isn't to try to find the nature or essence of justice, but to approach the problem of justice comparatively and to try to find criteria for an alternative being less unjust. (In this sense, for example, the abolishment of slavery in the US, Sen points out, wasn't based on any ideas about perfect justice, but comparative thinking.) An account of ideal justice, Sen argues, doesn't help to decide between two imperfect alternatives, because actual cases can diverge from the ideal in many ways, and the ideal doesn't specify any ways to compare or rank such departures from the ideal. (As he illustrates the point, if Mona Lisa is defined as an ideal picture, this tells us nothing about how to compare and rank a Picasso against a van Gogh.) Hence, the identification of an ideal is neither necessary nor sufficient for comparative judgments about justice. Indeed, the approach that aspires to define an ideal of justice may make discussion of actual non-ideal cases seem impossible. For, if justice requires ideal institutions then how can we, for instance, talk about global justice in current circumstances, when no ideal has been determined?

Finally, Sen points out, an important source of injustice seems to be behavioural transgressions rather than institutional shortcomings. For that reason too, focus on ideal institutions seems limited. The way in which Rawls' theory abstracts away from people's actual behaviour and talks about what 'reasonable people' would do, Sen maintains, is a simplification which is misleading from the point of view of practical reasoning about social justice. According to Sen, we have to look for institutions that *promote* justice, rather than treat them as manifestations of justice, as Rawls' theory does.

Further reading

Gaita, R. (2002), *A Common Humanity: Thinking about Love and Truth and Justice*. London: Routledge.

Sen, A. (2009), *The Idea of Justice*. London: Allen Lane.

Young, I. M. (1990), *Justice and the Politics of Difference*. Princeton: Princeton University Press.

Literature's ethical significance

The ethical significance of literature and its relevance for moral philosophy has been debated in analytic moral philosophy, especially since the late 1980s. How the significance of literature is understood is intimately connected with how the nature of moral deliberation and the tasks of moral philosophy are understood. On certain views literature plays no essential role, while according to others certain matters can be expressed adequately *only* in literary style, not in standard philosophical prose. Literature, of course, is a wide and diverse body of writing. The kind of literature that mostly gets discussed in this connection is fiction with clear narrative structure and detailed descriptions of characters and situations, as in the novels of Henry James and Jane Austen. Whether this focus reveals something essential about the issue, and whether this kind of literature is particularly relevant morally, isn't clear.

Why study literature and not real life? One reason is that our experiences are limited and literature has the capacity to expand on them. It can also enrich our understanding by making available multiple perspectives when describing how different characters perceive things and respond to situations, revealing to us their inner lives in ways that are not often available in real life. Another reason is that, although we may get emotionally engaged with characters in a novel and be variously affected by the situations described, we also retain a detachment from what is described in a literary text. That our own lives are not at stake makes us free of certain sources of distortion (such as hopes and fears relating to our own lives) that might blind us were we really part of what the text relates. Thus, the reader's role as an external observer makes it possible for her to learn about life through literature, and to use it to learn about herself, that is, her own habits of attention and perception, her own reactions, assumptions, attitudes and so on.

Regarding different conceptions of the relevance of literature, if one assumes that the task of philosophy is to spell out a theory of morality, or a standard or principle of moral evaluation that can guide our choices in particular circumstances, then the significance of literature looks something like the following. Characteristic of literature is its ability to describe examples and particular cases in much greater detail than philosophers can do in philosophical texts. Such vivid descriptions can then be used as support for philosophical theories or to express criticisms of them. From this point of view, literature constitutes, so to speak, an imaginary testing ground for philosophical theories and ideas. It enables us to examine in more concrete terms than an abstract philosophical text what particular moral philosophical views really amount to. For instance, it might be able to make apparent what it would be to live according to utilitarian principles and how this approach succeeds or fails to address the complexities of moral life. According to this conception, therefore, the moral significance of literature depends on the explicit or implicit arguments it may contain for or against theories, and on literature's illustrative powers. But although literary style and presentation may make issues strike us more forcefully, literature can't, on this view, ultimately say anything about morality that philosophical prose couldn't say, assuming we can understand the point and rational justification of philosophical theories and ideas independently of their literary illustrations. This means that literature can make no essential contribution to thinking about moral matters. It is merely a medium for the illustration of philosophical conceptions and arguments or a covert way of presenting arguments.

But it is important that what one might find morally significant in a literary text isn't independent of the moral philosophical approach assumed. For instance, a focus on choice and action in the manner of modern moral philosophical theories makes largely irrelevant the descriptions of the development of a person's character, psychological abilities such as perception and imagination, or specific attitudes, as found in a *Bildungsroman*, for example. On the other hand, such things might be perceived as directly relevant from the point of view of a virtue-ethical approach whose emphasis isn't on individual actions but on the moral agent's character, abilities and life, or if one seeks to approach moral philosophy from the angle of moral psychology. (*See,* METHODOLOGY, VIRTUE ETHICS.) Indeed, against this background, if seen as expressive of the characters' attitudes towards life, almost anything a text speaks about might emerge as potentially morally relevant. In this way the perception of relevance seems a function of the philosophical approach.

By contrast with the earlier conception of the significance of literature, Martha Nussbaum argues that there are moral views and facts about human life that can be adequately expressed only in the language and forms of literature. The study of relevant kind of novels therefore belongs within moral philosophy and a philosophical inquiry into ethics is incomplete without it.

The background of Nussbaum's view is her Aristotelian conception of the task of moral philosophy, moral deliberation and life. For Nussbaum the key question is 'How should one live one's life?' From this point of view the goal of moral philosophy emerges as the specification of what a good life is for a human being. But such a specification might quite naturally be taken to require more than the articulation of action-guiding principles. Discussion of skills, abilities, attitudes, motives, and so on, that make possible a good life, and a dialectical, juxtapositional examination of different conceptions of life, may be required to justify an account of how we should live.

According to this view, the relevance of literature isn't restricted to the illustration of ideas that could equally well be expressed in philosophical texts. For example, on Nussbaum's reading of Henry James' *The Golden Bowl*, the moral relevance of the text consists largely in how it can clarify to us matters relating to moral perception and responsiveness. But to describe how one may, for example, fail to be sufficiently attentive and responsive, what that may mean, and how such failures might be overcome, is a complicated task. As Nussbaum explains, *The Golden Bowl's* claims about value and imperfection would be very difficult to assess without the kind of sustained exploration of particular lives that James is engaged in, and without the support of a text such as his novel. In particular, according to Nussbaum, to show the correctness of the Aristotelian account of moral deliberation as something intuitive rather than a matter of following predetermined rules requires texts that make apparent the complexity, indeterminacy, and difficulty of moral choice. Importantly, a literary text also has available more resources than a standard philosophical text which it can use to bring across its points. It can appeal, not only to the intellect or reason, but also to our EMOTIONS and imagination. (*See*, EMOTIONS.)

Despite her view that moral philosophy requires the use of literary texts, however, Nussbaum's conception of the philosophical work literature can do seems to be philosophically fairly traditional. According to her, *The Golden Bowl*, contains an argument for the Aristotelian conception of moral deliberation, as well as, for example, a more specific argument about the inevitability of imperfections of moral perception. In this way the book aims to establish certain philosophical conclusions about the nature of moral deliberation. Nussbaum therefore appears to treat literature merely as a more advanced medium for the construction of arguments. But, one might ask, is that all literature can do for moral philosophy?

As Cora Diamond points out, one might, alternatively, treat a literary text, for example, not as a source of ideas about moral life, but as a stimulus for thinking. As she notes, a text can make us think without telling us what to think. Accordingly, Diamond is critical of Nussbaum's view that James' goal would be to provide us with answers about what the good life is, rather than laying out life for us to incite our thinking. In such a capacity literature might then, for instance, be able to broaden one's horizons by boosting one's imagination, thus making new ways of seeing things available and enabling more creative responses in moral situations. Hence, literature might be able to widen or deepen one's comprehension of moral matters. As Alice Crary explains it might be able to help one to develop one's sensibilities to the moral significance of something, such as certain character traits – for example, how pride may affect one's judgment. Or it might help one to realize the moral relevance of something by showing how things look from a particular point of view not directly available to one, such as that of a child. Understood in this way, literature may play an important role in a person's moral development.

Considering the ethical significance of literature, Diamond and Crary argue against the idea that the intellectual and affective dimensions of human life should be kept strictly apart. On a traditional philosophical view, EMOTIONS are non-rational or even irrational. Accordingly, rationality seems to require that moral persuasion must proceed by way of argument, appealing to the head rather than the heart. Nevertheless, one might argue against this traditional view, as Crary does, that it assumes a problematically narrow conception of rationality. Sometimes a clear perception of things may require emotional engagement, and not having an appropriate emotional response can signal a failure to understand something. Correspondingly, the way in which literature can emotionally engage us may constitute a rational mode of moral instruction. For example, an emotive response might draw one into a more intimate relation with a character in a literary work as opposed to other characters, and in this way lead to the recognition of certain features of life or qualities of persons that aren't available neutrally but only through emotional response. Through such a response one can then learn something about those qualities and their moral significance, and use this to make better sense of oneself. Notably, however, here moral instruction doesn't have the form of a judgment or conclusion established by way of argument. (When we learn something about morality through our emotional responses to a novel, what we learn isn't the conclusion of an argument.) Finally, literature might also be seen as significant for moral philosophy because it very clearly shows the moral significance of how things are described. It shows that how we describe things isn't morally neutral, and how moral views may be embodied in the concepts we use. (*See* THICK AND THIN MORAL CONCEPTS, EMOTIONS.)

Further reading

Adamson J., Freadman, R., Parker D. (eds) (1995), *Renegotiating Ethics in Literature, Philosophy and Theory*. Cambridge: Cambridge University Press.

Crary, A. (2007), *Beyond Moral Judgment*. Cambridge, MA: Harvard University Press.

Diamond, C (1991), 'Having a Rough Story about What Moral Philosophy Is', in *The Realistic Spirit*. Cambridge, MA: The MIT Press, 1991, pp. 367–381.

George, S. K. (ed.) (2005), *Ethics, Literature, and Theory: An Introductory Reader*. Lanham, MD: Rowman and Littlefield.

Nussbaum, M. (1990), *Love's Knowledge, Essays on Philosophy and Literature*. Oxford: Oxford University Press.

Metaethics

Metaethics is concerned with questions relating to morality that are theoretical rather than practical in any direct sense. Sometimes philosophers speak about a metaethical investigation as an inquiry concerning the logic of moral language use (or, in any case, used to do so in analytic philosophy before the 1970s). One might, however, also characterize metaethics as addressing metaphysical issues relating to morality (now that analytic philosophy has again become openly metaphysical). An example of a metaethical question is the question concerning the nature of moral judgments and whether they state something true or false. This question connects with other questions concerning moral properties such as, whether moral properties are properties that things (actions, and so on) genuinely possess, or perhaps something humans project onto things. Another example of a metaethical question is whether the possibility of moral discourse presupposes that there are moral principles, and what the role of principles is in moral thinking. (*See*, COGNITIVISM AND NON-COGNITIVISM, PARTICULARISM AND GENERALISM.)

As regards the significance of metaethical discussions for thinking about moral issues, philosophers such as Aristotle, Kant or Mill didn't explicitly draw any distinction between what philosophers nowadays call 'metaethics' and 'normative ethics'. (*See*, NORMATIVE ETHICS.) Rather than regarding metaethics and NORMATIVE ETHICS as sub-fields of moral philosophy, they apparently saw these two pursuits as different aspects of moral philosophy. Accordingly, given that questions concerning the nature of morality and moral thought may variously affect the (kinds of) normative claims philosophers make, these two aspects of moral philosophy appear ultimately intertwined. For example, Kant's conception of the independence of the foundation of morality from anything empirical and his goal of spelling out such a foundation for moral thought is both a reflection of and reflected in his view of the unconditionality of the commands of morality. (*See*, GROUNDWORK.)

By contrast, metaethics, as it has been practised in the twentieth century, has been mostly understood to be a value-neutral pursuit that has no direct moral implications for how we should morally judge some issue or another. (In part the rise of APPLIED ETHICS was a counter-reaction to this and the dominance of metaethics in analytic moral philosophy. *See*, APPLIED ETHICS.) But whether metaethics can be regarded as value neutral in this sense isn't clear. For example,

Richard Hare's assumption of the neutrality of the logic of moral language has been criticized by Iris Murdoch on the grounds that his views on the subject in fact embody liberal protestant views. Similarly, Jonathan Dancy, a leading contemporary proponent of metaethical particularism, maintains that the problem with the so-called generalism is ultimately a moral one. Generalism may lead one to insist on an unjust decision on the grounds of having made a similar decision in a different case, and invite neglect of the particular features of a case at hand. If this is correct, generalism would be an example of a case where metaethical assumptions regarding the form or nature of moral thinking are themselves a cause of moral mistakes. (*See*, PARTICULARISM AND GENERALISM.)

However, as the dispute between particularists and generalists may also be taken to illustrate, from the point of view of current metaethical debates, traditional theories make significant assumptions about the nature of moral thinking. There is a contrast here between Aristotelian VIRTUE ETHICS on the one hand, and Kantian and utilitarian ethics on the other, regarding the significance and role of moral principles. While Aristotelians tend to think that moral knowledge isn't codifiable in rules or principles, Kant explicitly sets out to analyse common moral understanding by reference to what he takes to be a fundamental principle underlying it. Similarly, Mill maintains that all moral deliberation ought to recognize as its basis the utility-principle which gives us an overarching, universal criterion for moral rightness. Here Kant and Mill implicitly adopt a generalists position in contrast to Aristotle's apparent particularism.

Further reading

Fisher, A. and Kirchin, S. (2006), *Arguing about Metaethics*. Abingdon: Routledge.

Miller, A. (2003), *An Introduction to Contemporary Metaethics*. Oxford: Polity Press.

Methodology

As elsewhere in philosophy, it is important in ethics not only to seek to directly address the issues one wants to understand, but also to think about what an appropriate way to approach them would be. There are many questions of this kind pertaining to philosophical methodology to consider, when attempting to comprehend the phenomenon of morality and how philosophy could help with moral matters. Three central questions are: (1) What concepts and issues should be the focus of the investigation? (2) What form should the investigation of such key concepts and issues take? (3) How should the goal of the investigation be understood from a practical point of view, or how to think about the practical relevance of moral philosophy? These questions have various interconnections, but let's discuss each in turn.

Regarding the first question, the focus of modern moral philosophy has been on determining our moral obligations or duties by establishing a cardinal moral principle posited as constitutive of the foundation of morality. ('Modern moral philosophy' means here Kantian and utilitarian ethics, which largely continue to dominate the mainstream of analytic moral philosophy.) Once established, the fundamental principle can then be relied on as a guide in moral deliberation, and used to justify moral judgments as well as further action-guiding principles. From the point of view of this approach, the central concept of moral philosophy is OBLIGATION or duty. The chief concern of moral philosophy is to determine what our obligations are and to decide questions of moral worth by reference to relevant moral principles. (*See*, OBLIGATION, DEONTOLOGICAL ETHICS, KANT, CONSEQUENTIALISM, *GROUNDWORK*, *UTILITARIANISM*.)

This approach contrasts with a different one represented, for example, by virtue ethicists. Here the focus of attention is not obligations and action-guiding principles. Rather, it is abilities that enable one to see clearly what morality requires, as well as the development of character, dispositions and other capacities that enable one to act accordingly. (*See*, VIRTUE ETHICS, NORMATIVE ETHICS, EMOTIONS.) But while the emphasis of VIRTUE ETHICS has been on so-called virtue concepts, this second type of approach might be understood more broadly as being concerned with moral psychology, that is, with the philosophical study of the mental capacities involved in moral agency, deliberation, perception and responsiveness. (*See also*, NATURALISM AND NON-NATURALISM.) From this point of view the sources of, for example, moral failures might then be sought, not in misconceptions about moral principles but, for example, in shortcomings in attentiveness, perhaps induced by blinding selfish biases.

Relating to the contrast between these two approaches questions about moral language also arise, for example, whether the focus of philosophical inquiry should be moral judgment-making and the nature of moral judgments, as opposed to the study of the ways in which evaluations are already embodied in how we choose our words when describing persons, actions, situations, and so on. That is, while it is characteristic of modern moral philosophy to understand moral language use as involving the employment of specific moral vocabulary, and to identify moral concerns by reference to a specific subject matter – the right or the good –, the representatives of the other approach (broadly understood) are more likely to envisage moral concerns as a ubiquitous dimension of human life and language. Thus, this approach assumes a significantly different picture of morality. (*See*, THICK AND THIN MORAL CONCEPTS, LITERATURE'S ETHICAL SIGNIFICANCE.) Indeed, it has been maintained, in opposition to modern moral philosophy, that the very term 'morality', understood as a system of moral principles, obscures a clear comprehension of the phenomenon of morality. As Bernard Williams and Iris Murdoch among others have argued, moral life is too complicated to be represented in the form of an overarching moral principle or principles. Other critics of modern moral philosophy and representatives of this alternative approach widely construed include Lawrence Blum, many Wittgensteinians such as G. E. M. Anscombe, Stanley Cavell, Alice Crary, Cora Diamond, Raimond Gaita, Lars Hertzberg, and Peter Winch, and often (but not always) virtue ethicists. Some similar emphases are also found in the work of Levinas. (*See*, LEVINAS.)

The last issue of whether it is possible to capture what is essential to moral life in terms of an underlying principle is connected with the second question above, concerning the form of philosophical accounts. (*See also*, PARTICULARISM AND GENERALISM.) Ever since Socrates, philosophy has largely assumed the form of the construction of philosophical theories, that is, the articulation of overarching definitions and explanations whose purpose is to capture what is common to all instances falling under concepts of philosophical interest, such as the concept of a morally worthy action, a virtuous person, moral judgment, and so on. In this sense, the task of philosophy has been seen as consisting in the pursuit of common essences underlying the apparent manifoldness of phenomena. Philosophy's goal, in other words, has been to spell out unified accounts that tell us what *all* cases falling under a concept *must* be, for example, what characteristics an action must have in order to qualify as morally worthy.

Philosophical theorizing (like science) commonly seeks generality, systematicity and economy. In this vein, consequentialists, for example, claim that the moral value of actions *always* depends on their consequences and Kantians that it *always* depends on the agent's motive. Mill expresses as follows the requirement that morality shouldn't merely be presented as an aggregate of prescriptions or principles, but systematically in the form of a unitary theory: '[. . .] there ought to be either some fundamental principle or law at the root of morality, or, if there should be several, there should be a determinate order of precedence among them; and the one principle, or the rule of deciding between the various principles when they conflict, ought to be self-evident.' (*Utilitarianism*, chapter 1, para. 3) As the quote shows, part of the hope for systematicity is that any conflicts between obligations, and so on, would turn out to be merely apparent. (*See*, NORMATIVE ETHICS.) Sometimes this hope takes the extreme form of the search for a decision procedure that would allow us to determine purely mechanically which actions would be right. (For this issue in relation to Kant-interpretation, *see* KANT.) Notably, although VIRTUE ETHICS is perhaps less systematic, the above characterization of philosophy as the search of an overarching theory applies to it too, insofar as its goal is to offer a unified and complete account of the nature of moral considerations and what it is to be a moral person. (For the systematicity issue, *see also* DEONTO-LOGICAL ETHICS.)

What philosophical theories seek to establish can be comprehended in more than one way. For example, Kant envisages his theory as a clarification of what we already know about right and wrong. His theory isn't meant to say anything new about morality, but just to give it a clear and defensible formulation. (*See*, GROUNDWORK.) Mill by contrast sees himself as a reformer improving on extant morality. This means, not simply helping us to live up to the requirements of morality that we already recognize, though may get confused about; the task is not merely to reform of our institutions, customs, practices, and so on, so that they accord with our moral commitments. Kantian clarification could also form the basis of a reform of this kind. Rather, Mill's project involves an idea of reforming morality itself, and developing it in certain ways.

(*See*, UTILITARIANISM.) Which one of these conceptions better explains the status of philosophical accounts isn't important merely for historical reasons, however, but because of the various offshoots these methodologies have in contemporary philosophy. For example, Harean investigations into the logic of moral language may be understood as a particular descendant Kantian *a priori* methodology. On the other hand, Harean logical or conceptual investigation seems to embody a very narrow conception of conceptual investigation by contrast to, for example, a Wittgensteinian conception of such an investigation. (Hare has been criticized for this narrowness by Williams who himself, however, seems to take it for granted that a conceptual investigation must be understood in such a narrow way.) The question here is, whether philosophical methodology can put us in a position where we can do justice to the richness of the facts of moral life, and avoid the abstractness and rigorism of Kant's *a priori* theorizing, while also avoiding problems in Millian empiricism.

An equally important question is whether morality and relevant moral concepts really possess the kind of simple unity philosophical theorizing assumes, which would make it possible to capture all cases falling under a concept in terms of a single definition. If this assumption about the nature of concepts or essences is problematic (as Wittgenstein argues in his later work), then philosophical theories that try to explain all cases that fall under a particular concept in terms of a single overarching definition or characterization run the risk of dogmatism and misleadingly simplifying the phenomena. In this sense the form of philosophical accounts might itself prevent us from achieving a clear comprehension of the manifold and complex phenomenon of morality or specific moral concepts. (*See*, GOOD, JUSTICE, RIGHTS, THICK AND THIN MORAL CONCEPTS, and CARE for examples of contexts in which this question arises.) If so, a different more piecemeal approach may be required that will enable us to do justice to the different aspects of moral concepts or different dimensions of morality, and doesn't assume uncritically that it is possible to capture our moral concepts in overarching definitions. As Hume notes in his *Treatise* (*see*, HUME), human nature is characterized by addiction to general rules as a consequence of which humans often carry maxims beyond the original reasons of their introduction. It seems crucial to avoid this problem in philosophy, and not to turn the rigour of the Socratic method of search for definitions into rigidity and lack of flexibility of philosophical thought. (For a discussion of such a methodology by reference to Wittgenstein, see further readings.)

Finally, relating to the third question regarding the practical relevance of philosophy, there is a further division that runs through moral philosophy (one that cuts across the dividing lines first discussed). The issue is whether morality necessarily requires self-examination whose purpose is to overcome any falsifying prejudices and biases, and to come to understand more clearly our moral commitments; or whether we can understand the task of moral philosophy legislatively, as laying down moral principles we ought to follow in moral life. The first conception is associated with Socrates and has been emphasized especially by Murdoch among contemporary philosophers. The second conception (with a little simplification) is assumed in Kantian and utilitarian ethics, but sometimes in VIRTUE ETHICS too. Again, depending on which one of these two approaches we assume, different conceptions of the tasks and nature of moral philosophy emerge. (*See,* APPLIED ETHICS, PERFECTIONISM.) But whatever the right conception may be, or however the Socratic and legislative conceptions might be integrated into one unified account of morality, it is important to consider this methodological question explicitly, rather than tacitly assuming one of these conceptions of philosophy's practical role and relevance. (*See also,* FREEDOM.)

Further reading

Kuusela, O. (2008), *The Struggle Against Dogmatism: Wittgenstein and the Concept of Philosophy.* Cambridge, MA: Harvard University Press.

Naturalism and non-naturalism

What it means to adopt (or not to adopt) a naturalistic outlook in ethics can be understood in different ways depending, on the one hand, on what one understands by 'natural' and, on the other hand, how the relation between the moral and the natural is construed.

A principled, though perhaps narrow, way to understand the natural is to identify natural terms with terms used in the sciences and natural properties as properties identified as such by the sciences, perhaps including psychology. Natural would then be, by definition, whatever the sciences treat, or will treat, as natural. This kind of naturalism can be understood purely methodologically, as merely involving a commitment to take as natural whatever the sciences identify as such. Naturalism in this sense need not involve any commitment to (putatively) *a priori* metaphysical claims about what belongs to nature – for instance, that nature is to be explained in terms of causal processes. But not all philosophers who call themselves 'naturalists' wish to identify the natural with what the sciences understand by natural, and construe the realm of natural more broadly. For example, one might regard human linguistic practices as something natural, though it isn't clear how and to what extent they might be scientifically explained and, more crucially, in what contexts of discourse such an explanation can contribute to rather than stand in the way of our understanding of the matters. (So far linguistics as the scientific study of language has had nothing to say about moral language use, and apparently shouldn't be expected to do so.) Depending on how strictly or loosely one defines the concept of the natural, one might alternatively run the risk of narrowness or vagueness.

Another way to understand the natural would be to associate it with the empirical, conceiving it as the object of synthetic statements and discoveries that result in new knowledge. A naturalist approach in this sense can be contrasted with a conceptual investigation, which doesn't aim to reveal anything new, but seeks to clarify concepts we use or to design new ones with the purpose of articulating ways of conceptualizing or presenting reality, and promoting philosophical perspicuity. Sometimes such an investigation is characterized as putting forward analytic statements, but such a conception doesn't capture conceptual investigation in a Wittgensteinian sense, which acknowledges that the empirical and logical are intertwined and not sharply separable. Notably, it is not clear that a conceptual investigation can be usefully distinguished from a naturalist investigation by reference to its object of investigation as opposed to methodology. A psychological study of, for example, EMOTIONS and a conceptual study of emotions (or moral psychology more broadly) may take as their objects the same phenomena, while approaching them in different ways. (See also, METHODOLOGY.)

Regarding the relation between the natural and moral, reductive naturalists seek to analyse moral judgments, concepts or predicates in terms of non-moral, natural judgments, concepts or predicates, or try to explain moral properties in terms of non-moral natural properties. A reductive explanation is one that allows, in effect, one to do without the terms or properties of the reduced level of discourse. Everything that needs to be said or explained can be said or explained by using the terms at the reducing level or by reference to properties at this level, which is perceived as more fundamental. (This isn't elimination in the sense that the reduced terms are recognized as speaking about something real.) By contrast, non-reductive naturalists maintain that moral properties can be understood as natural properties, but can't be reduced to any non-moral natural properties. Naturalists of this stripe may, for example, maintain that the relation between the natural and the moral is a supervenience relation. In the case of moral properties, their supervenience on the natural can be defined as follows: actions, characters and so on that are naturally identical, that is, identical when described in natural terms, are also morally identical. The supervenience thesis thus holds that, although the moral character of, for example, an action might not be identifiable on the basis of its non-moral natural properties alone, and therefore we might not be able to establish any moral classifications by solely looking at the natural level supervened upon, the descriptions at the two levels co-vary. That is, although an independent grasp of moral properties is required to establish correlations between moral and non-moral properties, a relevant difference in either level implies a difference at the other level.

An example of a non-reductive a theory is Philippa Foot's Aristotelian naturalism spelled out in her *Natural Goodness*. (Another example would be the so-called Cornell realists; see COGNITIVISM AND NON-COGNITIVISM.) According to Foot, the evaluations of human will and action share their logical structure with the evaluations of living beings in general. Thus, there is something like the GOOD of an x (for instance, an oak, owl, or a human being) determined by the facts pertaining to the life form in question. Such facts then constitute 'patterns of natural normativity' that determine what a flourishing being of the type x is like, and in the case of humans, how one ought to live in order to flourish. In the background of this idea lies an observation relating to a class of statements of the type 'a dog has four legs' which, although clearly factual, are not empirical generalizations. Rather, they are normative in a special sense, stating something like 'this is what a dog normally is or should be like'. (They are not normative in the sense of stating that in order for an animal to count as a dog it must have four legs. A dog who has lost a leg is still a dog, though it suffers from a defect.) According to Foot, morality is grounded, in this sense, on facts about human life. Despite the diversity of human life, it is possible, according to her, to find a ground in such facts for necessities relating to human life and well-being. However, rather than being intended as an account from which specific moral judgments can be derived, Foot's theory merely purports to clarify the foundation and status of moral judgments. She's talking about the framework in which moral disputes take place.

Depending on what exactly the reduction of moral terms to natural ones involves, naturalism may be understood in various ways. Reductivism may be definitional, that is, aiming to define moral terms in natural non-moral terms. This kind of naturalism is the target of Moore's open question argument. (*See*, PRINCIPIA ETHICA.) Alternatively, one might understand the reductive relation, not as a definitional a *priori* relation, but as a factual, synthetic relation. From this point of view, it would be a genuine discovery that, for instance, the property of moral goodness can be explained in terms of certain natural properties. Although Moore assumes Mill's naturalism to be definitional, it seems possible to interpret Mill differently, insofar as it is meant to be a discovery of psychology that the only thing people desire is pleasure and, consequently, that the maximizations of pleasure and minimization of pain is the criterion of moral goodness. (*See*, UTILITARIANISM.)

An example of a reductive naturalistic theory that is definitional, but might not fall prey to the open question argument, is Frank Jackson's and Philip Pettit's analytic moral functionalism. This theory attempts to find analytic, non-empirical links between moral terms and descriptive natural terms. The idea, however, isn't to find natural terms that are synonymous with individual moral predicates, that is, to define moral terms by natural terms one by one, or to reduce them to such terms term by term. Rather, it is to give a 'network analysis' of moral terms. The idea is that moral terms presuppose a network of connections with both evaluative and descriptive terms, and need to be characterized as part of such a network, through their relations with each other. More specifically, this characterization is given by stating what Jackson and Pettit call 'common places' about the relevant concepts. By this they mean platitudes about the concepts that are relevant for explaining them, for instance, to explain the inferential relations into which these concepts enter. An example of such common places is that a fair action is the one to be pursued, and that fairness has more justificatory power than politeness but less than the need to save someone's life. The statements of such common places are, according to Jackson and Pettit, *a priori* conceptual statements about the meaning of the relevant terms.

An example of non-naturalism is Moore's intuitionism. According to him, moral properties can't be defined in naturalistic terms, that is, terms of the natural sciences and psychology, as goodness is a non-natural property of natural objects grasped by moral intuition. (*See, Principia Ethica*) Although Moore's non-naturalism may seem mystifying because of the notion of intuition he employs, there needn't be anything particularly mysterious about his non-naturalism. It can be understood as merely holding that moral properties can't be reduced to natural properties, or that moral terms can't be reduced to natural terms. Rather, moral discourse is *sui generis*, constituting an autonomous level of discourse. (By comparison, few think that there is anything particularly strange about mathematics, even though the object of investigation of mathematics isn't natural objects, and mathematics can't be reduced to statements about natural objects.)

A contemporary representative of non-naturalism is John McDowell. The characterization of his position as non-naturalistic, doesn't mean that he would regard moral facts as supernatural. Rather, moral discourse is simply taken not to be explainable in natural, scientific terms. Moral competence and sensitivity to moral properties and facts are acquired through an upbringing into human practices and the development of conceptual capacities, that is, through a certain kind of education or formation. This education then gives rise to what McDowell calls 'second nature' which our moral sensibilities are part of. Insofar as this second nature arises through natural processes and is part of the life form of an animal with a language, there is nothing as such that contradicts naturalism in the broad sense of the word that contrasts with supernaturalism. Accordingly, McDowell's position is sometimes characterized as an extension of naturalism, a naturalism of second nature. Virtue-ethical outlooks that assume as their basis the McDowellian idea of second nature have been developed by Rosalind Hursthouse and Sabina Lovibond. Wittgenstein's philosophy, and especially his conception of language as a form of life, is sometimes assumed as a basis for naturalism in this sense. Yet another sense in which one might understand a naturalistic inquiry into morality is Nietzsche's natural history of morals. (*See*, Nietzsche.) Hume also offers a historical example of a naturalistic approach to the investigation of morality. (*See*, Hume.)

Further reading

Foot, P. (2001), *Natural Goodness*. Oxford: Oxford University Press.

Jackson, F. (2000), *From Metaphysics to Ethics: A Defence of Conceptual Analysis*. Oxford: Oxford University Press.

Jackson, F. and Pettit P. (1995), 'Moral Functionalism and Moral Motivation', *Philosophical Quarterly*, 45, (178), 20–40.

Miller, A. (2003), *An Introduction to Contemporary Metaethics*. Oxford: Polity Press.

Sayre-McCord, G. (ed.) (1988), *Essays in Moral Realism*. Ithaca, NY: Cornell University Press.

Schaber, P. (ed.) (2004), *Normativity and Naturalism*. Heusenstamm: Ontos.

Normative ethics

The goal of normative ethics is to determine the basis for answering questions about what is morally right or wrong, good or bad, what our obligations or RIGHTS are, how we should live, and so on. It seeks, in other words, to determine the ground or 'value-basis' for our regarding certain things as having moral worth as opposed to others. Through such determinations, normative ethics then also aims to provide guidance for action and choice. Traditionally, the focus of moral philosophers has largely been on issues we now classify as belonging to normative ethics. Nevertheless, it would be problematic to characterize the contributions of, for example, Aristotle, Kant or Mill to moral philosophy as restricted to normative ethics. Normative ethics, as the term is used in contemporary philosophy, contrasts with METAETHICS and APPLIED ETHICS. METAETHICS addresses questions of a more theoretical nature concerning moral concepts and the nature of moral thinking, while APPLIED ETHICS addresses questions relating to the practical consequences of philosophical theories of value. (See, APPLIED ETHICS, METAETHICS.) All three kinds of considerations can be found in the writings of the mentioned philosophers.

More specifically, there are two basic kinds of approaches to normative ethics. First, one may attempt to provide a systematic account of morality in terms of a fundamental principle or principles that determine what moral goodness or rightness consists in. Such a determination then further allows one to determine the moral value of particular actions, states of affairs, and so on. The attraction of a systematic account is that, if our moral valuations do indeed constitute a system, we would thereby know that our morality is consistent – or at least we would be in a position to examine this issue methodologically. Thus we might be able to establish that, moral tragedy doesn't exist in the sense of our morality driving us into situations of contradictory moral demands. A further hope is that this systematic account would also make it possible to generate a right answer to each morally problematic situation. However, it is less clear how the existing accounts of morality can make good this hope. Two leading moral philosophical theories that take this approach are Kantian deontologism and consequentialism: both put forward competing principles that aim to capture the foundation of morality. (See, DEONTOLOGICAL ETHICS, KANT, CONSEQUENTIALISM.)

Secondly, if one rejects the assumption that there should be a general overarching theory of moral value, expressible in terms of a principle or principles, one may alternatively seek to clarify the normative ground of morality in a more piecemeal fashion. Now the systematicity of morality isn't assumed, although not necessarily rejected either. Importantly, however, when the systematicity-assumption isn't made, the articulation of an overarching principle that constitutes the foundation of morality no longer emerges as a central goal, and philosophy assumes a different form. The prime example of this type of an approach is VIRTUE ETHICS whose emphasis is not on the evaluation of individual actions or states of affairs, but more broadly on what it is to be a good human being and what good life is. Unlike deontologism and consequentialism, virtue ethics characterizes the morally good or right in terms relating to the agent's character, deliberation and choice. The good or right isn't characterized in abstraction from moral agents by reference to the goal of morality (as in the case of consequentialism) or by reference to its *a priori* foundation (as Kant does). Instead, it is envisaged as an object of choice whose nature and identity become comprehensible, and that becomes attainable, through the development of certain abilities and dispositions. Accordingly, the characterization of those abilities and dispositions now becomes a central task. And while in the first type of approach the abstract characterization of the nature of morality or principle is put forward as a kind of tool for action-guidance, guidance is available in virtue ethics too, albeit in different form. It can provide action-guidance through its specification of the virtues and virtuous actions that one can then try to model one's actions on, and that constitute a guideline for progress towards virtue. (*See*, VIRTUE ETHICS, ARISTOTLE.)

Another way to characterize normative ethics is to distinguish it from ethics in a descriptive sense, that is, from the anthropological or sociological description of moral codes or systems of morality that people actually assume in particular places and times (such as Victorian morality). The contrast between normative ethics and ethics in this descriptive sense comes to view in that the principles put forward by Kant and Mill, for example, aim to capture, not simply the moral thinking of their times. Rather, the intent of both philosophers is to capture the underlying principle of morality with which any particular moral code or system ought to accord. Thus, instead of aiming to give a merely descriptive account of morality valid for a certain time and place, they seek to articulate an account of morality that is universally valid, and which we can use as the basis for the evaluation and justification of, not only particular actions, states of affairs, and so on, but also of particular moral codes or systems. (*See also*, RELATIVISM.)

Obligation

The concept of an obligation or a duty – of being bound, required or necessi-
tated by duty to do or not to do something – occupies a central place in
modern moral philosophy. In Kant's ethics, duty is the key concept in terms of
which the notion of a moral action and moral necessity is explained. According
to this view, humans as rational beings are under a general obligation to act
according to the moral law, from which more specific obligations then follow,
such as the obligation not to steal. Despite its differences from Kant's ethics,
the concept of obligation is equally important for utilitarianism. The core of
utilitarian ethics is a general obligation to advance utility (general happiness or
welfare). From this fundamental obligation, more specific obligations then follow, just as in Kant's ethics. (*See*, CONSEQUENTIALISM, *UTILITARIANISM*.) Thus, in both
Kantian and utilitarian ethics one might speak of two levels of duty: a fundamental level of duty to be moral, and a secondary level of specific duties. While
all moral action, according to these theories, assumes the fundamental level of
duty, what specific duties agents have is contingent upon the circumstances in
which they happen to find themselves. For example, if a Kantian subject lived
in a world where people had no concept of property, it would apparently
make no sense to attribute to her an obligation not to steal. However, to give
the concept of obligation or duty such a dominating role as it has had in modern ethics is perhaps also problematic in certain ways. Before going into that,
discussion of concepts and their relations is in order.

The concepts of obligation and duty may be characterized as normative or,
more specifically, deontological concepts, as opposed to value concepts, such
as GOOD and bad. (For the notion of deontology, *see* DEONTOLOGICAL ETHICS.) Other
central normative concepts are right and wrong which seem to presuppose a
norm that determines what counts as right or wrong. Thus, as G. E. M.
Anscombe notes, the concept of wrong belongs together with a law-based
conception of morality, and similarly also the concept of right. Here the norm
or law might or might not be explicitly formulated. For example, the starting
point of Kant's ethics is the observation that the normative foundation of
ethics requires clarification. It is just for this purpose that he seeks to find and
explicit formula for the underlying moral law. (*See*, *GROUNDWORK*.) Another
important normative concept is that of a right, which is closely connected
with obligation or duty. (*See*, RIGHTS and below.) What exactly the relation
between normative concepts and value concepts is, is a complicated question.

According to a standard account, primary for Kant is the notion of morally right in terms of which morally GOOD is then defined: to do what is right is GOOD. The order of determination in utilitarian ethics is the opposite. Now primary is the notion of moral goodness on the basis of which norms regarding the right conduct are defined: to do good is right. This may be correct as far as it goes, but doesn't clarify the relations of normative and value concepts generally.

Whether the concepts of obligation and duty are the same isn't clear and perhaps not definitely fixed. According to a broader usage (exemplified by Kant and Mill) duties and obligations are co-extensive (cover the same cases) or identical. According to a narrower usage, an obligation is something voluntarily accepted (e.g. promising creates an obligation) while duties are tied to the position, status, occupation or role of a person. (Presumably slaves have duties, though have not taken them on voluntarily; were men and women to have different duties on the basis of their sex, these wouldn't be voluntarily chosen.) On the other hand, the relations of the concept of obligation/duty, prohibition and permission, seem straightforward. When someone has a permission to do something, she lacks an obligation/duty not to do it or lacks a prohibition to do it. When someone has an obligation/duty to do something, she lacks the permission not to do it or has a prohibition not to do it.

The relation between the concepts of duty and right is a debated issue. In the case of what Kant and Mill call a 'perfect duty', the duty is owed to someone in particular, and one person's duty implies the right of another person. On the other hand, as Mill explains, in the case of imperfect duties, such as charity, although they are obligatory, the occasion of performing the duty is left to the agent's choice. Imperfect duties are not duties towards any people in particular or to be performed at any prescribed time. Accordingly, because no beneficiary is determined, imperfect duties don't give rise to RIGHTS, only perfect duties do. Sometimes Kant's conception of imperfect duty is characterized by saying that it doesn't prescribe a specific action, but an end. A special case is so-called duties towards oneself. Although in this case a beneficiary is apparently determined, the duty doesn't imply a right, insofar as one can't have a right against oneself. (Sometimes this case is explained away by saying that such duties *concern* oneself, though are not duties *to* oneself.) Somewhat loosely one might say that, while perfect duties are usually associated with negative, stringent duties not to do something, imperfect duties are associated with positive, less stringent duties.

As for possible problems with making obligation or duty *the* central and dominating moral concept, the question we need to ask is, what kind of a picture of moral life does the obligation-based view result in, and can it do justice to all relevant aspects of moral life? If the answer is negative, then rather than being understood as *the* central moral notion, we might do better to regard obligation or duty as only one concept among many, as Williams has urged. Let's turn to this.

Insofar as obligation or duty is assumed as the concept in terms of which we are to think about moral relations, then apparently, for example, an agent's relations towards people close to her, such as her children, should be characterized in terms of duties. And, of course, we do think that parents, in some cases at least, have duties towards their children. Further, the notion of such a duty might also be used to explain why a parent is permitted to pay special attention to her own children, rather than having to work indiscriminately for everyone's benefit, as the fundamental utilitarian duty would require. (*See*, IMPARTIALITY.) Indeed, in a certain way the assumption of this fundamental utilitarian duty forces us to think of, for example, parental relations in terms of duties, because once we start thinking about morality in terms of duties, only a duty is strong enough to override another duty. Any other reason for not doing one's duty, besides a more urgent duty, constitutes automatically a failure to act morally. However, this explanation also suggests that in the parent's case there are conflicting or rivalling duties one of which (namely, the duty to promote general welfare) isn't fulfilled. This seems problematic, because not doing one's duty or not taking care of one's obligations attracts blame. Yet, it would seem strange to say that the agent has in this case failed her obligation towards all other people of the world, even if only to take care of a more urgent obligation. The question, therefore, is whether an agent's moral relations to other people and actions should really always be explained in terms of duties?

One might try to avoid the problem of blaming parents for failing to their general utilitarian duty by saying that in a parents case the general duty is *transformed* into a parental duty and no duty is really left unfulfilled. This is so, one might argue, because for a parent the best way to contribute to general welfare is to take care of their own children. But what about the case where the agent simply wants to go to the cinema or a concert, and has no duty towards, for example, her own children that would override or transform the general utilitarian duty into a more specific duty? In this case there seems to be no duty that would release the agent from her fundamental duty to help everyone. If she doesn't have an obligation that beats the obligation to all the rest of the world, does that mean her obligation towards the world still holds? At this point the notion of a duty towards oneself might be brought into the discussion. For example, according to Kant, the moral agent has duties to herself because her own welfare is a condition for successfully taking care of her moral duties. (*See*, Kant.) Utilitarianism too allows that in order for moral agents to be able to effectively work towards the greater happiness of all, they must sometimes rest and relax. Thus, an agent's duty towards herself can override the duty towards the rest of the world, and all seems fine – although in this case it does seem that the agent has failed to do her general utilitarian duty, even if for understandable reasons. This should perhaps make us pause to think. Instead of assuming a duty towards oneself as an explanation for the permissibility of going to the cinema or a concert, shouldn't we perhaps look back and try to examine our apparent entanglement in duties. Should we really construe our moral relations to others and the world – ultimately everything we do that is approved by morality – in terms of duties?

Mill says in *Utilitarianism* that it is the task of moral philosophy to tell us what our duties are, or by what test we may know them (for instance, in cases where our duties seem to be in conflict). But if this is all, then it isn't a central task from the point of view of his ethics, for instance, to try to develop oneself, to try to come to understand and work on one's prejudices, attitudes and reactions, and so on. (*See*, methodology.) Rather, insofar as there is any need for self-development, then its goal is simply to be able to better know and more reliably do one's duty. In this sense utilitarianism, as well as Kantianism, makes other moral considerations subservient to duty or obligation. But does that do justice to what our moral lives really are like? Is moral failure always a matter of failing to do one's duty or would it sometimes perhaps be better characterized, for example, as blindness to how things are or what the salient moral features of a situation are? Rather than blame, couldn't the appropriate attitude sometimes then be, for instance, pity for a person in her blindness? And is moral necessity really always a matter of obligation?

Further reading

Anscombe, G. E. M. (1958), 'Modern Moral Philosophy', *Philosophy*, 33, 1–19.

O'Hear, A (ed.) (2004), *Modern Moral Philosophy*. Cambridge: Cambridge University Press.

Williams, B. (1985), 'Morality, the Peculiar Institution', in *Ethics and the Limits of Philosophy*. Cambridge, MA: Harvard University Press.

Particularism and generalism

The metaethical debate between particularists and generalists concerns the issue of whether principles must play a role in philosophical explanations of morality in either a practical or a theoretical sense. The practical question is, whether principles are required as guides in moral deliberation. The theoretical question is, whether principles must be assumed to explain the possibility of moral thought or to explain why the objects of moral evaluation possess the value they possess. In the latter case, principles might be characterized as articulating laws, so to speak, regarding the value-determining features of 'things' (actions, states of affairs, persons) that explain why, for example, certain kinds of actions are wrong, or why an instance of an action is wrong in certain circumstances. Thus, an action's wrongness might be explained, for instance, by reference to some specific wrong-making feature, such as that it is dishonest, which always or with certain qualifications makes an action wrong – however exactly the law is imagined. Alternatively, an action's wrongness might be explained in more abstract terms, for example along utilitarian lines, by it failing to contribute to the maximization of general happiness. Relevant laws might therefore be quite specific or highly general.

Traditionally, modern moral philosophy has assumed a generalist position, often on both questions distinguished before. For instance, utilitarians maintain that the utility-principle can serve as an action-guiding and/or a justificatory principle (which is to attribute a practical role to it in two different senses), and that it explains theoretically what makes and action right or wrong. Indeed, apparently Mill's view is that the principle can used for justificatory purposes *because* it captures an underlying law relating to human psychology and the concept of GOOD that is fundamental to morality. At the same time he maintains, however, that it would be impractical and psychologically unrealistic to assume that actual moral deliberation should always be explicitly guided by this principle. (*See, UTILITARIANISM.*) There are therefore several distinct roles principles might be taken to play in moral philosophy.

Particularists, on the other hand, deny that principles must figure in moral philosophical accounts in a practical or a theoretical role, although this isn't necessarily to maintain that principles can't be of any practical use in moral thought (see below). Jonathan Dancy, a leading representative of particularism writes: '[. . .] morality has no need for principles at all. Moral thought, moral judgment, and the possibility of moral distinctions—none of these depends in any way on the provision of a suitable supply of moral principles.' (Dancy 2004, 5) Thus, particularists argue that our grasp of moral situations doesn't have to be explained as based on moral principles that are either tacitly assumed or explicitly relied upon, and that moral deliberation isn't to be analysed in terms of such principles. Neither are principles or laws required to explain the existence of moral value.

The practical significance of moral principles, as understood in modern moral philosophy, may be further characterized as follows. The view that the determination of moral value must be based on principles, and that moral value can't be understood as something we are able to directly perceive or intuitively grasp, is connected with questions about the consistency, objectivity and rationality of moral discourse, as well as the justification of moral judgments. Regarding justification, if my judgments are based on my intuition/ perception and yours are based on yours, then in case of disagreement we seem merely to have our intuitions/perceptions to fall back on, and it is unclear whose intuition or perception should prevail. It is unclear, that is to say, how the dispute could be settled rationally, and in what sense moral judgments are objective, rather than merely express how things strike individuals. As for consistency, if my judgments are in each individual case based on some principle assumed as a standard of moral evaluation (or on principles that form a consistent system), then we seem to have a clear criterion for the consistency of judgments. My judgments are consistent insofar as they are based on the consistent application of a relevant principle or principles. By contrast, if there is no general standard of moral evaluation, it is less obvious how the consistency and objectivity of moral judgments is to be understood. I'll return shortly to the issues of justification and consistency from a particularist angle. Before that, however, a brief characterization of different generalist positions and their contrast with particularism is in order.

At its most extreme generalism might be understood as the view that moral thought is based on the mechanical application of principles or rules. To illustrate this, imagine an agent equipped with the principle 'Stealing is wrong' and a definition of stealing. On this basis, she might evaluate actions by making inferences of the following kind (in conformity with Aristotle's practical syllogism): (1). Major premise: Stealing is wrong. (2). Minor premise: This action constitutes stealing (or meets the definition of stealing). (3). Conclusion: This action is wrong. Of course, the idea of the mechanical application of rules can be readily problematized. Perhaps there isn't anything like establishing the second premise in a mechanical way, but judgment is required to determine where the definition applies, at least in complex cases. (*See also*, KANT and his notion of judgment and 'mother wit'.) However, a proponent of the principle-based view of moral judgment needn't adopt this mechanistic conception of moral judgment-making, and presumably there aren't many representatives of this extreme position. Nevertheless, even if the application of principles requires judgment, one might still maintain that moral judgments necessarily involve moral principles. For example, Aristotle, might be attributed this kind of view, insofar as he maintains that moral judgment requires practical wisdom which involves both knowledge of a universal principle (major premise) and knowledge of a particular acquired through experience (minor premise). (*See*, NICOMACHEAN ETHICS.) Note also that it isn't necessary to construe the generalist position according to the previous model of deductive reasoning which is used here for illustration. Principle-based thinking may take various forms.

Aristotle is sometimes also interpreted differently from the preceding, for example, by McDowell and some other proponents of VIRTUE ETHICS. (*See*, VIRTUE ETHICS.) Instead, Aristotle is taken to reject the idea that moral knowledge involves any principles at all. According to this view, the goal of the virtuous person is to act in such a way that her actions will constitute a *eudaimonic* or a happy life. But what constitutes such a life can't be captured in any definition or codified in principles or rules. Understood in this way, moral deliberation and action would therefore not be based on the application of *any* rules or principles. Rather, as McDowell describes the virtuous person, she knows occasion by occasion what to do, not by applying universal principles but being a certain kind of person who sees situations in a certain distinctive way. This Aristotelian position is sometimes taken as a prototype for particularism.

By contrast to the generalist account of justification above, particularism can offer its own account of the justification of moral judgments. From this perspective disputes about moral issues can be understood as disputes about what the salient or morally relevant features of the situations in question are, this being ultimately something to be decided case by case. To support her judgment of a case, the particularist can, for example, refer to similarities and differences between cases. The point of such comparisons is that they can help one to see the case under discussion more clearly; in other words, they can be used to clarify the relevance of some of the features of the case. Here the appeal to another case, however, isn't to be understood as based on the principle that since feature x made such a contribution to the situation in some other case, it must make it here too. Instead, the idea is that a simple and more perspicuous case can help one to better understand a more complicated one. Notably, this kind of a way of justifying moral-judgments doesn't normally constitute anything like a conclusive proof. Rather than being a weakness of the particularist account, however, one might regard it as bringing to view something characteristic of moral disputes. Often they tend to be less straightforward to solve than factual disputes.

This contrast can be further elucidated by contrasting a generalist and a particularist analysis of the statement: 'That is stealing and therefore wrong.' In the light of generalism the statement might be analysed as something like the following inference. (1). Stealing is wrong. (2). That action constitutes stealing. (3). Conclusion: That action is wrong. (Note, however, that generalism does allow that the principle of the first premise is something much more specific, and has built in into it qualifications relating to cases in which stealing is wrong.) Alternatively, from a particularist perspective the statement could be analysed along following lines. The reason why this act is wrong is that it constitutes stealing, whereby that is a morally relevant feature of the act; it is that which makes the action wrong (in this particular context). Analysed in this way the statement has no implicit inferential structure. It doesn't constitute an inference or an argument, and it isn't based on a principle about the wrongness of stealing. Here moral understanding is seen as more akin to perception than inference.

As regards the rationality and consistency of moral judgments, particularists can point out against generalists that although it is true that rationality requires consistency, it isn't true that consistency requires codifiability of moral knowledge in principles. What consistency requires is that we don't hold contradictory beliefs or make contradictory judgments. This, however, doesn't require that the judgments must be based on a principle (or principles) that cover all similar cases and by reference to which they are to be judged. Consistency merely requires that, insofar as we are to judge two similar cases differently, there must be some morally relevant difference or differences between them. (Similar considerations apply in the case of objectivity.)

The last point is connected with Dancy's argument for particularism. According to him, particularism is intimately connected with holism about reasons, which is a view about the sensitivity of reasons to context. For example, a consideration that constitutes a reason for doing a certain action in a certain context might not be reason for doing it in another context, or might even be a reason against it. Holism also says that reasons don't necessarily combine additively. There might be a case where two features that on their own would constitute a reason for action don't constitute a reason for action when combined. Hence, according to holism, a feature that is right-making (or duty-inducing, and so on) in some contexts need not be right-making in all contexts, but can be neutral or a wrong-making in other contexts. For instance, that an action is a lie can make it either cowardly or brave, depending on how we imagine the circumstances. It can therefore be something that ought to be done or ought to be avoided.

Holism about reasons stands in contrast with atomism about reasons, which Dancy depicts as holding that what is a reason to do (or not to do) a certain action in one situation is always a reason to do (or not to do) the action. This means, for example, that if being an act of lying is a wrong-making feature of actions, then an action's being an act of lying is always a reason not to do it – or at least another reason is needed to make this action acceptable, that is, to balance out the wrongness of lying. In principle, however, the feature of being an act of lying always contributes to the moral value of the action in the same way, whether balanced out by other features or not. This contribution could then be captured in a principle.

Holism about reasons contradicts this view of the invariance of reasons. Even though invariance might be true of some cases, it's mostly false, Dancy maintains. And while a principle-based conception of morality, according to him, is incompatible with holism about moral reasons, holism about moral reasons is compatible with there being some invariant moral reasons. Invariant reasons, however, should be regarded as invariant because of their specific content, not because reasons must always be invariant. Thus, Dancy's view isn't that there are no considerations that always make something morally forbidden. (For example a murder might always be wrong.) Rather, the view is that moral reasons needn't be invariant. More specifically, according to particularism, the possibility of moral thinking doesn't depend on there being invariant reasons specifiable in terms of principles. If moral reasons are holistic, Dancy maintains, this gives a reason (though not a conclusive one) to think their possibility isn't based on there being principles we rely on in moral thinking.

Nevertheless, generalists have more than one counter argument. First, one might seek to reject holism about reasons, and argue that the impression of their holistic behaviour is merely a consequence of the incompleteness of the explanations or justifications we give. A generalist, in other words, might respond to the holistic/particularist conception of moral reasons or right-making features by making the principles more complex. Now a relevant principle isn't simply, for instance, that one has promised; the principle doesn't consists of treating promising on its own as duty-inducing feature. Rather it is that one has promised, keeping the promise isn't immoral, the promise wasn't given under duress, and so on. Thus, one might maintain that, if we take all the reasons together, they can guarantee, for example, the rightness of an action. Nevertheless, there are problems with this response. Lists of that seek to enumerate negative features such as the mentioned will become very complex, if they are to account for all the relevant features, and are in danger of becoming unmanageable. A more serious problem is – given that a generalist needn't assume moral principles to be manageable and to function as guides but can ascribe to them a merely theoretical role – that such lists seem to be, in effect, infinite. In other words, there seems to be no principled way of stopping adding qualifying reasons. If so, the generalist response can't turn the dialectic to their benefit. A principle for which there is no formulation is merely an imaginary principle. (By contrast, Dancy suggests treating features such as that a promise wasn't made under duress as 'enabling conditions'. That one isn't under duress isn't by itself a reason to do anything, and should not be taken to function as such, when part of a complex reason.)

Another response is for generalists to embrace rather than seek to deny holism about reasons. A way to do this is to assume relevant principles to be qualified or hedged in such a way that they can accommodate the kind of context-dependence of reasons Dancy describes. Arguments of this type, which avoid the problem of the infinity of qualifications, have been recently put forward by Sean McKeever and Michael Ridge as well as Pekka Väyrynen.

A highly significant consequence of particularism, if it is correct, is that if moral deliberation can't be captured in rules, then morality can't be systematized or captured in a system of rules, unlike Kantian and utilitarian ethics assume. Here it is also relevant that, despite their opposition to moral principles, many particularists would grant some practical role to moral principles, for example, in moral education, as summaries of moral knowledge, or as heuristic rules of thumb. Principles might also be used in disputes to point out similarities and differences between cases, – although from a particularist perspective, a principle can't be taken to assert that a feature highlighted by the principle must *always* be regarded as relevant for moral evaluation.

Further reading

Dancy, J. (2004), *Ethics without Principles*. Oxford: Oxford University Press.

Hooker, B. and Little, M. (eds) (2000), *Moral Particularism*. Oxford: Oxford University Press.

McDowell, J. (1998), 'Virtue and Reason', in *Mind, Value and Reality*. Cambridge, MA: Harvard University Press, pp. 50–73.

McKeever, S. and Ridge, M. (2009), *Principle Ethics: Generalism as a Regulative Ideal*. Oxford: Oxford University Press.

McNaughton, D. (1988), *Moral Vision: An Introduction to Ethics*. Oxford: Blackwell.

Väyrynen, P. (2006), 'Moral Generalism: Enjoy in Moderation'. *Ethics*, 116, 707–741.

Perfectionism

Hilary Putnam suggests a distinction between two species of moral philosophers: legislators and perfectionists. While the former seek to provide us with moral rules, the latter, although they don't deny the value of rules, insist on something prior to this without which the rules will be worthless. This is the need to ask, what kind of life one should live and what kind of a person one should be or try to become, and to strive towards moral perfection. Moral perfectionism thus involves an existential commitment that goes beyond what any system of rules could provide: a demand for self-examination, moral development through self-knowledge, and responsibility, which may require the transformation of oneself or the society. This responsibility for one's actions and life, and for the kind of person one is, is one that can't be handed over to anyone or anything else, as if one could rely in one's life and actions on the advice of moral experts, safe in the belief that doing what the experts say or conforming to some moral code is enough. (*See*, APPLIED ETHICS.)

The classification of philosophers as perfectionists and non-perfectionists isn't straightforward, because a perfectionist dimension can also be found in thinkers whose work is generally more of the legislating and moralistic type. Broadly conceived, perfectionists include, for example, ARISTOTLE, KANT, MILL, NIETZSCHE, WITTGENSTEIN, HEIDEGGER, LEVINAS, FOUCAULT and CAVELL. Perfectionism finds an expression, for instance, in Socrates' concern for the 'welfare of the soul'. (*See*, SOCRATES.)

Perfectionism can be understood in more than one way. It can be envisaged teleologically as a matter of striving towards a particular goal, a standard of moral perfection, as, for example, encapsulated in an account of a fully developed human nature. JUSTICE as the state of one's soul, as discussed by Plato in REPUBLIC, and virtuous life in Aristotle are examples of attempts to determine such a goal. Taken in this way, perfectionism involves the identification of a specific state or a set of characteristics, for example, certain skills and motivational dispositions, which one ought to develop and acquire. The assumption of such a standard of achievement, however, brings teleological perfectionism close to legislative moral philosophy, and its conception of moral evaluation as based on some fixed standards of morality. Alternatively, perfectionism (in the sense of what Cavell calls 'Emersonian perfectionism') can be understood as not involving a commitment to or favouring some particular way of life over others. Rather, it is a matter of searching for direction and liberation, trying to understand where one stands, for example, what justice is and what kind of a person one must become in order to properly comprehend what justice is. Seen in this way perfectionism is a process of perfecting oneself rather than attaining some predetermined goal of perfection. Thus, attainment of a new state and a self might never be the attainment of a final, 'perfected self'.

Another question relating to perfectionism concerns the issue of whether perfectionism is inherently anti-democratic or elitist. Although there might be grounds for reading Nietzsche as affirming such a view, as Rawls writes in *A Theory of Justice* (§50), Cavell has argued that this need not be the case. Not only is perfectionism compatible with democracy but democracy positively needs it.

Further reading

Cavell, S. (1990), *Conditions Handsome and Unhandsome: The Constitution of Emersonian Perfectionism*. Chicago: University of Chicago Press.
Hurka, T. (1993), *Perfectionism*. New York: Oxford University Press.
Putnam, H. (2002), 'Levinas and Judaism', in S. Critchley and R. Bernasconi (eds) *The Cambridge Companion to Levinas*. Cambridge: Cambridge University Press, pp. 33–62.

Relativism

Moral relativism is a conception of the status and nature of morality, or the status of moral practices or systems. Relativists deny that there are any objective moral standards or norms in the strong sense that certain standards or norms ought to be universally accepted by everyone. Relativism thus rejects the more traditional absolutist conception of morality, according to which there is one true or correct morality that everyone should accept and respect. While philosophers have traditionally sought to find a foundation of morality in either facts relating to the external nature or to human nature, or perhaps even assumed moral standards to be God given, relativists typically view morality as based on human customs, that is, as conventional and thus arbitrary to an extent. Often, anthropological observations regarding different moral practices have served as the starting point for relativistic considerations.

Moral relativism assumes that there are or can be different, in principle equally acceptable, systems of morality or different moral practices. But it isn't simply the view that moral practices actually diverge. Various conclusions might be drawn from actual moral diversity, and it doesn't as such imply relativism (see below). Rather, what characterizes relativism is the claim that there is no objective, neutral or superior point of view from which to arbitrate, or no neutral criteria by which to decide, which moral practices or systems are right. This amounts to saying that there isn't anything like a correct or true morality. For, if it is impossible in principle to compare moral systems or practices with respect to their correctness, then it doesn't make any sense to say that one is correct and another one incorrect, or one more correct than another one. Rather, the relativist says, when we talk about the correctness of a moral view or judgment, we are doing so in the context of some moral system or another that constitutes a background – some kind of a framework of values – for particular moral judgments. The correctness of moral judgments then is relative to such frameworks. Consequently, a judgment might be correct in relation to some framework and incorrect in relation to another. The frameworks themselves, however, aren't correct or incorrect (or one isn't more correct than another).

Relativism comes in various forms. Protagoras in Plato's *Theaetetus* holds a subjectivist view, according to which man is the measure of things. According to this conception, whatever way things appear to be to a person, that is how they are for that person. What is true therefore is relative to a judging subject; what is true for you, might not be true for me. Cultural moral relativism, on the other hand, holds that standards of value are determined by cultural practices, and that each culture should, accordingly, be judged by its own standards. If we judge other cultures by our own standards, we are guilty of 'ethnocentrism'; we unfairly judge them by standards that are not their own.

What could be said in support of relativism? The view that there is no single correct morality is sometimes presented as an explanation of the actual diversity of moral practices and systems that exists. That the diversity exists, according to this explanation, reflects the fact that there isn't any correct morality. In this way the relativistic thesis then seems able to explain certain aspects of reality to us. A related argument asserts relativism to follow from the actual diversity of moral practices or systems. That actual diversity exists, according to this argument, shows the truth of relativism. Crucially for both arguments, however, the correctness of relativism can't be demonstrated by reference to actual moral diversity. Actual diversity might equally well indicate that some moral practices or systems are wrong, or that certain people are mistaken about moral matters. Perhaps the others, or we ourselves, are simply callous, cruel, selfish or thoughtless, for instance, and the moral disagreement between us and the others merely testifies to the moral shortcomings of one or more of the disputing parties. Actual moral diversity therefore is compatible both with relativism and absolutism. Indeed, if actual diversity weren't in principle compatible with absolutism, it would be difficult to understand the point of any traditional philosophical attempts to justify certain moral standards, or even the everyday practice of justifying particular moral judgments. Such justifications can only have a point – or even seem to have a point – on the assumption that people can diverge in moral matters, while someone is right and someone else wrong.

But what if even the 'thoughtful and well-educated' disagree on some fundamental issue, due to no carelessness or morally questionable motives? Would this show that relativism is true? A problem with this move is that what is recognized or regarded as thoughtful, for instance, might not be entirely neutral. Perhaps those whom we perceive as thoughtful are just those who agree with us, and our exclusion of some view or someone as thoughtless merely reveals our moral disagreement with those who hold that view. If so, the introduction of terms such as 'thoughtful' or 'thoughtless', and so on, doesn't make it possible to resolve the dispute about relativism, and moral disagreements as such don't suffice to show that relativism is correct.

It is also notable that relativism doesn't necessarily require that moral diversity actually exists. Ultimately, the relativist claim only seems to be that there *could* be different moral practices, and that there aren't any neutral grounds to decide between them. (It might be that all people contingently happened to agree in their moral practices, even though morality doesn't have any object-ive foundation in the sense rejected by relativists.) Thus, relativism seems best understood as a thesis about the nature of morality which is independent of any questions of actual moral differences. Understood in this way it might be construed as asserting that moral views are acquired, not through a rational fact-finding process (like scientific views), but through a non-rational process of enculturation. Consequently, moral views aren't something true or false, and there is no neutral point of view from which other cultures could be criticized.

Moral relativism is sometimes recommended on the grounds that it is tolerant; it is an expression of respect for different moral views. (Accordingly, relativism might seem attractive on the historical background of European colonialism, for example.) However, the problem with this way of supporting relativism is that, when adopted as a general principle, relativism may require one to tolerate what ought not to be tolerated, for example, intolerable cruelties. Thus, tolerance doesn't seem to necessarily possess any positive moral value, or perhaps better, its relation to mere indifference requires clari-fication. Accordingly, rather than adopting the overarching principle that everything should be tolerated, it would seem preferable to retain the option to decide in particular cases, whether something ought to be tolerated or not. How this could be done in a non-arbitrary manner that doesn't involve simply declaring one moral framework to be the correct one – and begging the question against the relativist – is a question that calls for an answer.

An issue to be raised in connection with the dispute between relativism and absolutism is, whether we can really assume that these two positions are the only ones available and that we really must choose between them? Could both views perhaps be problematic as accounts of the nature or morality, so that the dispute between them really has its roots in the way philosophers think about morality? Notable in this regard, as observed by John Cook, is that both relativism and absolutism seem to regard morality as a system or collection of moral principles that determine what is GOOD, right, and so on. This view appears problematic, however, in that if what is good or right is thought of as determined by such principles, were someone to disagree with some such principle, there seems to be nothing further to support it. That is, if the wrongness of, for instance, stealing, unfairness, and dishonesty is determined by principles such as 'stealing is wrong' and 'unfairness is wrong' then should someone question the wrongness of stealing, an explanation such as 'because it is unfair' or 'because it is dishonest' adds nothing to what the principle already states. 'All' that seems left to do then is merely repeating the principle or the relevant moral conviction. But this makes morality look arbitrary just in the way relativism claims it to be. (Certain further Kantian or utilitarian moves might be attempted at this point, but it isn't certain that they can solve the problem, and for reasons of concision I will not discuss them here.)

Would it help, if instead we thought about morality in terms of more specific value terms, such as 'cruel', 'callous', 'selfish', and so on? (*See*, THICK AND THIN MORAL CONCEPTS.) When I perceive something as cruel or selfish my perception appears informed by the relevant concepts. Otherwise it would seem difficult to explain my comprehension of relevant distinctions, such as that between cruelty and callousness. Crucially, however, such concepts may demonstrate cultural variation, and consequently this conception too may seem to lead to relativism. For, if concepts are conventional, then presumably value concepts are conventional, and therefore they too must be arbitrary.

But is it true that morality is simply conventional, as, for example, Gilbert Harman maintains? Or should morality be seen as having some kind of a factual basis, that is, as based on facts about human beings or their environment? Here we face, once again, the disputed question whether relativism or absolutism is correct. For the question about the conventionality versus factuality of morality is simply a more specific formulation of that same question. On the other hand, however, one might reject both accounts as unsatisfactory, insofar as they are presented as exclusive explanations of the nature of morality. First, the problem with the account of morality as something purely conventional is that it seems to force us to conceive all moral views as equally acceptable or leads to nihilism, the denial that anything really has value. (Conventions may vary, but when they do, who is right? Perhaps no one is, but all are on equal footing. But does that mean that value isn't anything real, a mere human fiction?) Secondly, the problem with trying to derive morality from facts relating to human beings and/or their surroundings is that there isn't any straightforward way to derive value judgments from facts and, in particular, to account for the unconditionality of the demands of morality on this basis. (*See*, COGNITIVISM AND NON-COGNITIVISM, KANT.) As a response to these difficulties, one might perhaps maintain, instead, that morality has to do with both the conventional and factual; that in the case of morality the conventional and factual are intertwined. Neither aspect is reducible·to the other one, but both are needed in order to explain the nature of morality.

To outline this conception very briefly, compare moral practices to those relating to food. The kind of food people eat in different places and times differs significantly. People may be absolutely disgusted by others culinary customs and would refuse to eat some foods or couldn't do so even if they tried. Such customs seem conventional. Nevertheless, nowhere do people eat pebbles or sticks or pieces of glass. This has to do with facts about humans, about what they can digest and use as food. It is also a fact that some food is healthier than others; some lead to bad health and don't promote well-being. Perhaps morality should then be seen as on analogy with our practices relating to food. Although there is room for variation, not all practices lead to well-being or can sustain a good life, just as not all practices relating to food can support a healthy life. If so, what is GOOD (and so on) isn't merely a matter of convention. Rather, the space within which conventions may vary is limited by facts about humans and their environment. This would then also mean that not all moral systems or practices need be regarded as equally acceptable. (*See also*, NATURALISM AND NON-NATURALISM.)

Further reading

Cook, J. W. (1999), *Morality and Cultural Differences*. Oxford: Oxford University Press.

Harman, G. and Thomson, J. J. (1996), *Moral Relativism and Moral Objectivity*. Oxford: Blackwell.

Moser, P. K. and Carson, T. L. (eds) (2001), *Moral Relativism: A Reader*. Oxford: Oxford University Press.

Rights

The nature of rights is a long disputed topic. Rights might be characterized as entitlements, but there are also other views, which we'll return to. Rights as entitlements may entitle one to a variety of different kinds of 'objects'. For instance, there are rights to do or not to do something, rights to be or not to be in some state, rights that others do or not do something or be or not be in certain states, and rights to 'things', such as one's body. Notably, moral rights are only one type of right; there are also legal, political and customary rights. The borderlines between these different types of rights are not clear-cut and the types overlap. For example, a political right might simultaneously be a moral right and have a legal basis enforced by law. The concept of a right is connected with that of a duty. Often, though not always, someone's right implies a duty to someone else. (*See*, OBLIGATION.)

The concept of a right has a particular history. There is a discussion whether the ancient Greeks had such a notion at all, given their language didn't possess a corresponding word. However, they clearly recognized rights such as right to property, and part of the population enjoyed political rights. Plato's REPUBLIC starts with a discussion of a suggested definition of JUSTICE as giving everyone their due that also seems to involve the recognition of rights. Part of the history the notion of rights is a development from rights being claimed by the powerful (as in a King's divine right to rule) to the current situation where it is common for social minorities or the oppressed to use the notion of a right to defend themselves and to redress injustices. Traditionally, rights are regarded in philosophy as something an individual can possess. More recently, there is also discussion of group rights, that is, rights belonging to a group rather than its members separately. An example is a group's right to self-determination. Another recent debate is whether animals have rights.

Regarding the nature of rights, there are two main theories, the will or choice theory and the interest theory. These theories both seek to explain the nature of rights in terms of their function or role, that is, by reference to what rights do for their possessor and how rights determine the right-holder's relations with other persons or groups. According to the will theory, represented, for example, by Kant and more recently by H. L. A. Hart and Hillel Steiner, a right gives the right-holder a power or discretion over someone's duty. A right, in other words, puts the right-holder in a position to control what the person

bound by the corresponding duty must or must not do in certain circumstances. For example, a promise gives the right-holder not only the right to
expect the fulfilment of the promise but also to waive it.

The will theory has certain weaknesses, however. It entails that there are no
rights over which the possessor has no power. Yet, under the current laws
I don't have a right to waive or annul my right not to be enslaved. That is,
I don't have the power to decide whether to uphold or release someone from
her duty not to enslave me. But this lack of power means that, from the point
of view of the will theory, I don't have a right against being enslaved. Another
weakness is that the will theory can't explain the rights of those who can't
exercise them or use the powers they give, for example, infants.

According to the interest theory, on the other hand, the function of rights is
that they protect or advance the interests of their possessor. Rights are, in this
sense, defenders of the well-being of the right-holder, which accounts for
why they are normally good to have. An advantage of this account is that it
makes it possible to explain the rights of infants, and the right not to be
enslaved. Clearly, these rights protect or advance the interests or well-being
or their possessor. The interest theory is represented by, for example, Bentham
and Mill, and among contemporary philosophers, David Lyons, Neil MacCor-
mick, and Joseph Raz.

Nevertheless, the interest theory has problems of its own. A problem with
characterizing rights as something that benefits or furthers the interests of
the right-holder is that there are rights that don't do that. For example, in the
case of many occupational rights, it is unclear how whatever the occupation
entitles a person to do, for instance, to enter burning houses to save people,
benefits the person herself. Similarly, a promise might sometimes serve the
purpose of benefitting the promise maker rather than the promisee. An
example is making someone promise to stop smoking. An interest as such,
of course, doesn't give anyone a right either. If so, interests are apparently
neither necessary nor sufficient for rights.

The debate between these two theories appears to have come to a standoff,
where neither party is able to emerge as the winner. Each side aspires to put
forward an overarching account of the function of rights that covers all
instances of moral rights from the point of view of their favoured normative
theory (deontologism or consequentialism). In so doing, both parties seem to

end up simplifying matters in problematic ways. Rather than successfully capturing the concept of a moral right as a whole, both theories seem in effect to emphasize particular aspects of it, while failing to account for some other aspects. Partly, the complexity of the concept that comes to view here might be explained by reference to its complicated history. At different points the concept has been used for different purposes and has been developed accordingly. The result is a concept stretched to serve many functions and that can't be explained with reference to one such function only, as Leif Wenar has argued. A. I. Melden expresses a similarly sceptical view of the traditional theories' prospects of success, maintaining that there is no single concept and single definition of moral rights. Rather, he maintains, the term is a so-called cluster concept.

Responding to this state of the debate, Wenar has proposed an alternative account, according to which, rights have several functions or roles, including but not restricted to discretion over someone's duty and protecting the right-holder from harm. This alternative theory is based (with certain modifications) on an account of rights by lawyer Wesley N. Hohfeld in the early twentieth century. Hohfeld proposed an account of rights as analysable into different separable elements, the so-called Hohfeldian incidents. Analysed in terms of these incidents, rights such as freedom of speech, for instance, turn out to be complexes of incidents. However, the system of Hohfeldian incidents also allows the generation of non-existent rights, such as immunity against a power that doesn't exist. (The Hohfeldian system implies a corresponding immunity right in each case where there is an inability to do something.) On the other hand, when the Hohfeldian incidents are coupled with Wenar's account of the functions of rights, so that in each case a right also serves a particular function, the problem of the generation of non-existent rights seems solved. Rights that are not recognized as rights don't serve any function either of which Wenar identifies six.

To briefly explain, the Hohfeldian incidents are specified, first, in terms of two primary rules that determine two incidents: the privilege right (or liberty or licence) and claim right. Secondly, there are two secondary rules which specify two further incidents: power right and immunity right. The latter two can be used to introduce new rights or to modify the status of existing rights. Rights specified in this way can then be arranged in tables that make perspicuous their relations. The six functions specified by Wenar are: exemption (from a general duty), discretion (regarding a general duty), protection (e.g. from harm), provision (in case of need), performance (of what has been promised, for example), and authority (in the case of a power right).

From the point of view of the Hohfeld-Wenar account, there isn't then any one characteristic common to all rights, contra the will and interest theories. Rather, rights may combine various Hohfeldian incidents and functions. Crucially, due to its greater complexity, the Hohfeld-Wenar model seems better able to explain the nature of rights than either the will or interest theory alone. The analysis of rights in terms of Hohfeld's incidents also readily clarifies issues such as whether rights always imply a corresponding duty. In Hohfeld's model, the correlate of a claim-right is a duty. The correlate of an immunity-right, however, is incapability (lack of power), which differs from a duty. Hence, rights don't always correspond to others' duties.

Another debate relating to rights concerns the issue of who can have rights and what the basis or justification of the attribution of rights is. According to the so-called status theories, humans have certain characteristics that make possible the ascription of rights to them. Proposed characteristics are rationality, free will, autonomy and personhood, or having a capacity to regulate one's life in accordance with a conception of the good life. The status-based approach is connected with the will theory of rights. According to the mentioned kind of criteria, right-holders are capable of choice and therefore of exercising the powers that rights give. A contemporary representative of the status-based approach is Robert Nozick. The so-called instrumentalist theories, on the other hand, regard rights as means to achieve certain distributions of interest satisfaction or utility maximization. This approach is connected with the interest theory. From this point of view the justification of rights is regarded instrumentally in the sense that the recognition of right-holders' rights is seen as a means to achieve the goals of morality that are specified independently of the notion of rights. A common form of instrumentalism is rule-utilitarianism. Mill's own view is close to this in that he regards the justification of social institutions, such as the rules of JUSTICE and rights, in terms of their utility. (*See,* CONSEQUENTIALISM, *UTILITARIANISM.*)

An objection to instrumentalism is that it makes rights fragile. If it turned out that the violation of certain rights would be the best way to maximize utility, then this would be what ought to be done, according to utilitarianism. In this sense the instrumentalist conception of the moral status of a person differs significantly from that of the status-theory. While according to the instrumentalist view there are no inviolable rights, the status-theory can assign inviolable or absolute rights to right-holders. Unlike instrumentalism, it regards the possession of certain rights as part of being a certain kind of being, not merely as a means to a further end.

A related issue is whether rights require social recognition and maintenance, or whether they can be had independently of their recognition by society. According to Mill, for instance, rights do require recognition. As he explains, to have a right is to have a sufficient or valid claim to something guaranteed by society. In this view, having a right requires two things: that a claim is made and that it is recognized as valid by the society. It isn't entirely clear how literally Mill understands the notion of a claim. Perhaps he doesn't regard rights as requiring that an explicit claim is actually made in cases such as the rights of infants against violence. However that may be, such a literal view (represented for example by Joel Feinberg) seems to give rise to problems, insofar as it places intellectual demands on right-holders that are high enough to exclude, for example, infants. Moreover, the conception that the existence of rights is conditional upon their recognition seems problematic in cases such as the rights of slaves. Should those rights really be regarded as conditional to their recognition, so that if a slave doesn't have a conception of her rights, or agrees with the owner that she doesn't have any rights, she therefore has no rights? By contrast, the status-theories hold that no recognition is required for the existence of a right. This dissolves the problem with the recognition-dependence of rights, and the problem that one needs to be able to make a claim in order to have a right. On the other hand, as explained, the criteria by which the status theories assign rights are somewhat restricted, excluding beings that are not capable of exercise their rights.

Further reading

Edmundson, W. A. (2004), *An Introduction to Rights*. Cambridge: Cambridge University Press.

McCloskey, H. J. (1965), 'Rights', *Philosophical Quarterly,* 15, 115–127.

Melden, A. I. (1988), *Rights in Moral Lives*. Berkeley: University of California Press.

Wenar, L. (2005), 'The Nature of Rights', *Philosophy and Public Affairs*, 33, (3), 223–253.

Stoic ethics

The Stoic school was influential in the Hellenistic period and in the early period of the Roman Empire. Its representatives include its founders Zeno (334–262 BC), Cleanthes (331–232 BC), Chrysippus (c. 280–c. 206 BC), and later on Seneca (1–4 BC–65 AD) Epictetus (55–135 AD) and Marcus Aurelius (121–180 AD). Stoicism was an influence on thinkers such as Michel Montaigne, Blaise Pascal, Baruch Spinoza and Kant.

Characteristic of Stoic ethics is its concrete practical orientation: the purpose of philosophy is to enable one to lead a happy and a good life and not merely to talk about it. Thus, Epictetus, for example, emphasizes that the discussion of theoretical philosophical matters should only be the last stage of philosophical study. First, one should try to get one's life in order through the study of proper objects of desire as well as the practice of appropriate actions and the application of principles. The study of logic, however, is regarded as very important for ethics too. Without knowledge of logic one may be easily misled. Similarly, physics as the third field of philosophical study is taken to be intimately connected with ethics. Physics describes reality as a law-governed whole in which everything has its place and with which one should live in harmony.

From the Stoic perspective, a principal cause of unhappiness is our desire for and aversion to things that are outside the sphere of our choice or beyond our power and control. This results in unrest and worry. Someone who doesn't get what she desires is unfortunate, and someone who incurs an object of her aversion experiences misfortune. The only things that are ultimately within our control are our own judgments and choice, including actions dependent on choice (opinions, impulses, reactions, desires and aversions). On the other hand, things such as health, wealth, death, and other people are outside our control. According to the Stoic view, only what is within our control is GOOD or EVIL. What is outside our power is neither good nor evil but indifferent. For example, death might be judged to be something good or evil, but it isn't good or evil as such. Accordingly, although no one can escape death, correct judgment may enable one to escape the dread of death, and live happily.

In the Stoic view, virtue consists of actions that exhibit the right kind of focus on what is in our power, that is, that exhibit correct judgment and choice.

Virtue constitutes human happiness, or what is characteristically good for human beings, and it is the only really good thing. Happiness, therefore, is identified with the possession of virtue. More specifically, an ideally virtuous person is someone who is in control of what is in her power, thus achieving independence from what isn't in her power. Consequently, such a person is free, cheerful, just, and so on. Whatever might happen to her, nothing can harm her: a good man/person can't be harmed. Progress towards virtue is possible through the practice of philosophy and by performing correct actions.

More specifically, as Epictetus explains this view, although we have natural preconceptions of the good as something advantageous, and happiness as something desirable, we may go wrong in applying these preconceptions in particular cases. In this way we may mistake as good something that isn't really good. What we therefore need to do is to examine our impressions of things with respect to their correctness, that is, to examine whether the way things appear to us is really the way they are, before we assent to the impressions and act on them. Crucially, humans are capable of such an examination as rational beings. More concretely, as regards the examination of our impressions by Stoic writers, their discussions often assume a therapeutic form. This consists in the philosopher trying to show the interlocutor a way out of her false beliefs that cause distress and to change the way she looks at things. One way in which the Stoics attempt to modify our impressions and to change our attitudes is through the re-description of situations. For example, life is described as a festival or party to which we are invited and death as a door that is always open for us to leave. And when the time has finally come to leave, would it not be rude towards the host to insist on staying?

Finally, although it is characteristic of Stoicism that it teaches us to accept as they are things that lie beyond our power, this doesn't mean that Stoics recommended inaction or fatalism. Nothing in the Stoic view implies that one shouldn't act to promote ends one judges to be worth promoting. Rather, the point is that whatever the ultimate outcome of one's actions, one should accept it with the right kind of attitude. This can be explained in terms of Chrysippus' response to the so-called Lazy Argument: does it follow from the Stoic view that, in case I fall ill, I shouldn't seek medical help, but should accept that I will either die or recover from my illness as my fate is? No: for it might be that my fate is to recover *because* I sought medical help. Similarly, it would be incorrect to think that Stoicism urges one to submit to oppressors rather than to oppose them. It speaks about the attitude with which to do whatever one judges as the right thing to do.

Further reading

Epictetus (1995), *The Discourses of Epictetus*. C. Gill (ed.), translation revised by Hard, R. London: Everyman.

Long, A. A. (2002), *Epictetus: A Stoic and Socratic Guide to Life*. Oxford: Oxford University Press.

Long, A. A. and Sedley, D. N. (eds) (1987), *The Hellenistic Philosophers: Translations of the Principal Sources with Philosophical Commentary*, Vol. 1. Cambridge: Cambridge University Press.

Thick and thin moral concepts

A debate in analytic moral philosophy concerns the distinction between so-called thick and thin moral concepts. Thin concepts are abstract, general moral concepts such as good/bad, right/wrong and ought. Examples of thick concepts are rude, brutal, kind and courageous. They might be characterized as more substantial or as having more specific descriptive content than their abstract cousins, and as being thick in this analogous sense. A notion related to that of thick concepts, though broader, is Iris Murdoch's 'specialized' moral concepts. R. M. Hare speaks in relevant contexts about 'secondarily evaluative' concepts in contrast to 'primarily evaluative'. The terms 'thick' and 'thin' were originally introduced by Bernard Williams. Key issues in the debate are how to explain the nature and function of thick concepts, and what their significance is for moral philosophy.

The origin of the debate goes back to the 1950s, with attempts by Philippa Foot and Iris Murdoch to challenge the so-called fact and value distinction in a sense that excludes the logical possibility of deriving value statements from descriptive statements of fact. (In another formulation, the distinction excludes the derivation of action-guiding ought-statements from descriptive is-statements about how things are. The distinction can also be construed in other ways.) Thick concepts, however, combine both a descriptive and evaluative dimension in a manner that seems not to fit the fact-value distinction – especially if it is intended as a division of statements or concepts into two exclusive categories. As Williams puts it, thick concepts seem to express a union of fact and value. Similarly, Murdoch maintains that our perceptions and descriptions of reality in terms of the specialized moral concepts are already morally coloured, rather than anything neutral. Foot sought to make use of examples such as the concept of rude in defence of naturalism against non-cognitivism, which maintains that value judgments are not descriptive of reality or according to which the primary function of value judgments is not descriptive but rather expressive of moral sentiments of approval and disapproval. (*See*, COGNITIVISM AND NON-COGNITIVISM.)

As a response to the challenge by Foot and Murdoch, R. M. Hare argues that the meaning of evaluative concepts is made up of two logically distinct components, the prescriptive (evaluative) and descriptive (non-evaluative) meaning. (*See*, COGNITIVISM AND NON-COGNITIVISM). According to him, the difference between the (later thus nominated) thick and thin moral concepts is that in the case of thin concepts the prescriptive meaning is primary and more firmly attached to the word than the descriptive meaning. In the case of thick concepts, by contrast, the prescriptive meaning is secondary, and more easily detachable from the descriptive meaning. Hence, according to Hare, it is merely accidental that we don't have a descriptively equivalent but morally neutral concept for courageous, for example. We could have one. However, if the evaluative dimension is thus detachable from the concept of courage, then it isn't essential to it. What Hare's argument therefore aims to establish is that concepts such as courageous don't themselves have any inherent evaluative force. They only possess evaluative force because we tacitly assume moral principles such as 'courage is good' in their use. The real evaluative work therefore is done by the thin non-descriptive concepts, a comprehension of which underlies the use of thick concepts. And since we could, in principle, adopt different moral principles, there isn't anything good about courage as such, or no such evaluation is built-in into the concept itself. (Simon Blackburn puts forward a different argument similarly designed to explain away thick concepts and their significance.)

Hare's argument, in turn, has been contested by pointing out that it problematically assumes our concepts to be detachable from the life in which they are embedded in the sense that we could, for example, continue identifying certain actions as courageous on the same descriptive grounds as previously, but attach a different value to them. But it is not easy to make sense of this suggestion if it means, for instance, that while continuing to connect courage with heroic actions, and regarding courage often as a precondition for such actions (all of this identified 'purely descriptively'), we would celebrate the heroes and the results of their actions, but view negatively the courageous way of performing those actions. Thus, as Foot pointed out against Hare, is it really plausible that we can simply decide what counts as benefit and harm, as Hare's argument appears to assume? However, how we are to explain the evaluative content of thick concepts and its connection with descriptive content remain disputed issues.

Regarding the significance of thick concepts beyond issues relating to the fact-value distinction, if it is possible to explain the function of thick concepts without reducing them to thin ones, then thick concepts also bear relevance to the question of the possibility of a general theory of moral value. It is the thin concepts that are at the centre of attempts to spell out such a general theory, whose goal is to give an explanation of moral goodness or rightness that covers all relevant cases. But if thick concepts are not reducible to thin ones, then it is unclear in how far a general theory of thin concepts can explain what we overall understand by moral value. Indeed, should the thick concepts turn out to be required to give content to the thin concepts in particular cases (as in characterizing something as wrong because it is unfair), that is, should the thick concepts ultimately turn out to do the evaluative work after all, then the prospects of an overarching theory of value seem even dimmer. (Murdoch, for example, maintains that all the work of primary evaluative terms could be done by the secondary ones.) Apparently nobody wants to suggest that such a theory of value could or should take the form of a pluralistic combined theory of rudeness, braveness, thoughtlessness, boringness, and so on for all thick concepts. (This wouldn't really even seem like a theory in any readily recognizable sense; see METHODOLOGY.) In this connection it is also noteworthy that, by contrast to the moderns, the ancients didn't focus on the thin concepts, or aspire to define moral value in an abstract, general way. They were content to talk about morality in terms of thick virtue concepts such as JUSTICE, courage, and so on. It isn't obvious why this should constitute a defect or a lacuna in their thought.

Finally, thick concepts can interestingly also be used to illustrate Murdoch's idea of moral differences as conceptual differences, and thereby used to throw light on some complexities relating to moral disagreements. It is part of this conception that moral disagreement can sometimes take the form of, not only contesting the correctness of a moral judgment, but also of contesting concepts employed in making the judgment, and the appropriateness of the judgment in this different sense. For example, one might not only disagree that sex outside marriage is sinful, but disagree with the use of sinful as an evaluative notion in the first place. Thus, in the case of morality there can be disagreements on several levels, not just about the correctness of judgments but also about the concepts employed therein.

Further reading

Blackburn, S. (1992), 'Through Thick and Thin'. *Proceedings of the Aristotelian Society, Supplementary Vol.* 66, 284–299.
Foot, P. (2002), 'Moral Arguments', in *Virtues and Vices and Other Essays in Moral Philosophy*. Oxford: Oxford University Press.

Gibbard, A. (1992), 'Thick Concepts and Warrant for Feelings'. *Proceedings of the Aristotelian Society, Supplementary Vol.* 66, 267–283.

Hare, R. M. (1963), *Freedom and Reason.* Oxford: Oxford University Press. (Chapters 2 and 10.)

Murdoch, I. (1998), 'Vision and Choice in Morality', in *Existentialists and Mystics.* New York: Penguin Books.

Williams, B. (1985), *Ethics and the Limits of Philosophy.* Cambridge, MA: Harvard University Press. (Chapters 7 and 8.)

Universalizability

The requirement of universalizability is often taken to spell out a key characteristic of moral judgments. Even if universalizability is not sufficient to explain what makes a judgment a moral one, it may nevertheless be regarded as necessary for a judgment to qualify as moral. This view is held by Kant, for example, and following him R. M. Hare. (*See*, GROUNDWORK; for Hare's theory, *see* COGNITIVISM AND NON-COGNITIVISM.) If the requirement of universalizability articulates a necessary condition for moral judgments, it may be said to be part of the logic and essence of moral judgments that they are universal.

What the universalizability requirement demands more specifically is that moral considerations (ought to) apply in the same way in each similar case (whereby the notion of similarity, however, can be construed in more than one way). For example, if morality requires a particular agent to do X in certain circumstances, it must require this from any other relevantly similar agent in relevantly similar circumstances. And more generally, universalizability requires one to judge each relevantly similar agent, action, state of affairs, and so on, in the same way. Thus spelt out, the requirement seems to capture certain important features of morality: that (1) moral judgments should be objective in the sense of not being merely the expression of personal preferences randomly followed; morality requires consistency. And (2) morality excludes favouritism and double-standards; any difference in how we morally judge a case assumes a morally relevant difference pertaining to the object of such considerations. Here mere numerical differences aren't enough, and thus the requirement excludes a different treatment of you and me simply on the grounds that I'm me and you're you, in the absence of any other relevant difference. (*See*, IMPARTIALITY.)

In order to understand what the universality of moral judgments means, it is important to distinguish universality from generality. (Often enough these notions are not clearly distinguished. There are also established everyday uses of 'universal' that ignore the difference, for example, 'universal healthcare' in the sense of healthcare available to all generally.) The difference between universality and generality is that a universal principle can be highly specific and still completely universal. Given its specificity, the use of such a principle might lack any generality, perhaps applying only in a particular single case. As this illustrates, generality contrasts with specificity. Universality, on the other hand, contrasts with particularity and singularity. That a universal moral principle with no generality might not be a very useful guide for moral deliberation, due to lack of opportunities to employ it, brings to view a certain on-going negotiation between the requirement of universality and the aspiration for generality that informs the type of moral philosophy whose goal is to spell out action-guiding principles. (See, METHODOLOGY.) Generality can be achieved at the expense of specificity, but should not be allowed to obscure morally relevant differences.

Formally, the requirement of the universalizability of moral judgments leaves open just what counts as a relevant similarity and thus what licenses the application of a principle or a judgment. This means that the requirement doesn't exclude the possibility of treating people in morally problematic ways with reference to characteristics that would not normally be considered as morally licensing such treatment. For example, it is compatible with the universalizability requirement to discriminate on the basis of sex or race, as long as the treatment is consistent and universal, that is, if the discriminatory principle is applied without exception whenever the sexist or racist criterion is met. This shows that universality alone isn't sufficient for a judgment to qualify as moral.

But it isn't clear that universalizability is a necessary characteristic of moral judgments either. For morality seems to permit me to require more from myself than from others, and yet there might not be any morally relevant difference between you and me in such a case, except me being me and you being you. Morality therefore seems to leave room for certain asymmetry of its requirements that depends on who is speaking, so to say. Although I can require more from myself than from others, others can't similarly require more from me than themselves (in the absence of some relevant difference). They can only require more from themselves. Thus, the moral agent seems to enjoy a special relationship to herself which licences her to exempt herself from the universalizability requirement to the benefit of others. This isn't compatible with the requirement of universalizability formally understood. Rather, if we want to hold on to the requirement that moral judgments should necessarily be universalizable, then the special relation that an agent enjoys with herself must be made part of the account of moral judgments, and their asymmetry explained in this way. However, if one now takes this asymmetry to be a characteristic of the logic of moral judgments, then their logic is morally contentful. The recognition of the asymmetry as part of the logic of moral judgments is a recognition of it as morally relevant, but it isn't recognizable as such from a purely formal point of view.

Further reading

Hare, R. M. (1981), *Moral Thinking: It's Levels, Method and Point*. Oxford: Oxford University Press. (Chapter 6.)

Mackie, J. L. (1977), 'Universalization', in *Ethics: Inventing Right and Wrong*. London: Penguin Books, pp. 83–102.

Winch, P., (1972), 'The Universalizability of Moral Judgments', in *Ethics and Action*. London: Routledge, pp. 151–170.

Virtue ethics

Virtue ethics was the dominant form of ethical theory in ancient and medieval times, but fell into marginality in the modern period. It has experienced a revival in the last few decades and has now become the third big theory, besides utilitarianism and Kantian ethics. While Aristotle is the greatest influence on contemporary virtue ethics, this doesn't mean that virtue ethics today is Aristotelian in every respect. For example, not all contemporary representatives subscribe to Aristotle's monistic and teleological eudaimonism, according to which *eudaimonia* or happiness is the only thing valuable in itself, and the value of everything else is relative to happiness. That is, not all virtue ethicists maintain that the value of the virtues or a virtuous character derives from their making it possible for an individual to reach happiness, or their being constitutive of such a life. Contemporary representatives of eudaimonism include Rosalind Hursthouse and John McDowell, while Michael Slote and Christine Swanton take up a pluralistic view of moral value. (*See also*, ARISTOTLE and *NICOMACHEAN ETHICS*.)

The reason for the re-emergence of virtue ethics seems mainly dissatisfaction with Kantian ethics and utilitarianism, both of which largely ignore, for example, issues relating to moral education, moral character and the relevance of EMOTIONS to morality. (*See*, EMOTIONS.) Possibly this passing over means not only that some relevant issues are left out of discussion, but that some important resources for understanding the phenomenon of morality are left out of the picture. Historically speaking, a turning point was G. E. M Anscombe's article 'Modern Moral Philosophy' that has been widely interpreted as urging a return to virtue ethics, consequent to its criticism of Kantian and utilitarian ethics. While the interpretation of Anscombe's article might be open to discussion, a reading of this kind seems to inform, for instance, Alasdair MacIntyre's *After Virtue*, the first contemporary book-length treatment of virtue ethics.

What is characteristic of virtue ethics? It isn't enough to define this approach to say that it acknowledges the moral importance of virtues. Virtues play a role in Kantian ethics and utilitarianism too, although for them virtues are, roughly, a means to an independently given goal. They are seen as character traits that facilitate moral action, or even make one do more than could normally be morally required. Kantians and utilitarians, however, determine what counts as moral action without any reference to the concept of virtue and in terms of their respective fundamental principles. These principles then constitute the foundation of morality for utilitarians and Kantians in the sense that they provide a criterion of moral worth and a basis for the derivation of moral obligations. Accordingly, the value of virtue too is to be determined in the light of these principles. (See, CONSEQUENTIALISM and KANT.) For virtue ethics, however, it is the virtues that constitute the foundation of morality. The morally good or right isn't determined in terms of some overarching moral principle, but good or right is whatever is virtuous or whatever the virtuous person would choose. In this way, the morally good and right are identified by reference to the virtues.

In a certain sense, the focus of virtue ethics, therefore, is the moral agent's character, and this theory is agent-centred, rather than rule- or consequences-centred. However, that its focus is on the agent or character needn't be taken to imply that virtue ethics has nothing to say about individual actions or, to use a term central to modern theories, that it can't offer action guidance. Definitions have been offered, for instance, by Hursthouse and Swanton, that seek to define the criterion for the rightness of actions in terms of virtue concepts or what the virtuous agent would do. Virtue terms have also been argued, by Slote, to be able to justify moral duties or obligations.

A question relating to attempts to provide a virtue-based definition of the rightness of action is, whether it is satisfactory to define right action exclusively in terms of what a virtuous agent would do. A potential problem here is that when the rightness of action is defined by reference to how the virtuous agent would act, what counts as right action begins to look arbitrary: whatever the virtuous agent takes to be right is now regarded as right. What seems missing here is an explanation of the sense in which what is morally valuable is independent of what someone happens to think or do. In other words, a criterion for moral worth is needed that is independent of what anyone in particular takes to be morally valuable. Accordingly, it has been suggested that what is distinctive about a virtuous person is that she is responsive or sensitive to certain features or aspects of reality which the non-virtuous person fails to respond to, and which (for the virtuous person) constitute a reason for reacting in a particular way to the situation. Now reality itself is thought to provide the required kind of independent test for the correctness of moral judgment and action. Another way to respond to the problem might be to clarify the status of the virtuous agent as an ideal model for how we ought to live, not to be confused with any actual agent.

Another potential problem arises in connection with attempts to offer action guidance in terms of virtue-based rules, such as 'act honestly' or 'do what a honest person would do'. The question is: if the correct application of virtue based rules requires that one should be virtuous, what help are such rules to a person who isn't already virtuous? And if one is already virtuous, then presumably one doesn't need the rules. Hence, it seems unclear who could benefit from such rules. More specifically, it may be difficult to know, for example, what honesty requires in certain circumstances. Does it merely require telling the truth, or also not keeping a secret? What do I do, for instance, in a situation where the virtue-based rules about honesty and, say, sensitivity conflict? A priority ranking of virtues and virtue-based rules might solve the problem. But it isn't clear that such a ranking can be given. The question here is whether the moral knowledge of the virtuous person can be codified in rules, that is, whether this knowledge can be stated in the form of principles whose application could be understood even by the non-virtuous person. Both McDowell and Hursthouse reject this idea of codifiability. (Similarly Aristotle emphasizes that knowing what is good requires becoming good. (*See,* NICOMACHEAN ETHICS.)) What this entails is that virtue-based rules can't constitute anything like a decision procedure that enables one to solve any moral problems purely mechanically. Beyond this negative outcome, however, it isn't entirely clear how the role of virtue-based rules should be understood.

As regards moral motivation, virtue ethics suggests that acting with proper moral motivation should be regarded as a matter of acting from a virtuous character. What exactly this means might be specified in more than one way, but presumably it includes, among other things, having appropriate kind of emotional responses and attitudes. (*See also,* EMOTIONS.) Notably, insofar as proper moral motivation is something that requires the possession of a virtuous character, morally motivated action seems impossible, for example, for children who have not yet developed the appropriate kind of character. Similarly, this view seems to exclude there being something like a single isolated morally motivated and morally right action by a particular agent. From this point of view, ascribing moral motivation is something that goes beyond the moment of action and it isn't a matter of attributing to the agent some occurrent state that accompanies her action. Interestingly, insofar as the notion of an ideally virtuous agent is used to characterize what moral motivation is, the moral motivation of actual agents may also be seen as a gradual matter, depending to what degree they approximate the ideal virtuous agent. Similarly, an action's possessing moral worth might then not be regarded as an all-or-nothing matter. For example, although the person who acts with inappropriate feelings may act in a morally right way in principle, one might say that the actions of the person with appropriate feelings are morally better. (Hursthouse's example is a person who takes pleasure in revealing some hurtful truth rather than regretting the necessity.)

But if virtues and moral sensitivity is acquired through initiation into social practices, does that mean that what is right/wrong or good/bad is simply determined by the society into which one happens to be born? In other words, does virtue ethics lead to conservativism or RELATIVISM? (*See*, RELATIVISM.) Aristotle himself held that reflection on human nature allows us to determine which practices are good. Nowadays many view such claims about human nature with suspicion, however, and for example MacIntyre's virtue ethics is relativistic. It isn't clear that relativistic conclusions need to follow, however. Sabina Lovibond argues that being a rational moral agent involves the possibility of questioning the practices within which one has been brought up. Thus, one isn't required simply to accept the values of one's society and a 'dissent morality' is therefore possible.

Further reading

Crisp, R. and Slote, M. (eds) (1997), *Virtue Ethics*. Oxford: Oxford University Press.

Hursthouse, R. (1999), *On Virtue Ethics*. Oxford: Oxford University Press.

Lovibond, S. (2002), *Ethical Formation*. Cambridge, MA: Cambridge University Press.

MacIntyre, A. (1984), *After Virtue* (second edn). Notre Dame: University of Indiana Press.

Swanton, C. (2003), *Virtue Ethics: A Pluralistic View*. Oxford: Oxford University Press.

The Key Thinkers

Aristotle

The ethical thought of Aristotle (384–322 BC) remains highly influential to this day, and is the strongest single influence on contemporary VIRTUE ETHICS. (*See*, VIRTUE ETHICS.) Beyond antiquity, Aristotle's ethics played an important role in the middle ages, and was developed especially by Thomas Aquinas to suit Christianity. (*See*, GOD AND RELIGION.) Unlike modern ethical theories (Kantian ethics and utilitarianism) whose focus is on the evaluation of actions, Aristotle regards as the central ethical issues the way one should live one's life and the development of a character and characteristics that enable one to live well, in accordance with the GOOD of a human being. The Aristotelian conception of human good is spelt out in terms of the concept of *eudaimonia*, often trans-lated as 'happiness'. However, *eudaimonia* doesn't mean happiness in the sense of a transient state of consciousness. Rather, it means living well or suc-cessfully. Thus, it might also be rendered as success, well-being, fulfilment or human flourishing.

What matters for happiness, according to Aristotle, are certain kinds of activities or living one's life in a particular way. (For example, a life spent asleep isn't a happy one, no matter how good one's character is. In order for a life to be successful it must be lived.) Moreover, in order for a life to qualify as happy, happiness must be a permanent characteristic of it, covering a person's life as a whole. Thus, for example, a life that ends tragically would not count as happy. Possibly even events after one's death may affect the characterization of one's life as happy, for instance, if one's life's work is destroyed or rendered futile. Unlike the Stoics, Aristotle regards fortunes and external goods as part of a happy life, though they are complementary rather than absolutely essen-tial to it. (*See*, STOIC ETHICS.) It is difficult to lead a virtuous and a happy life without resources – for instance, friends, wealth and political influence. Because of their association with successful life such things are sometimes confused with happiness. But they are not identical with it. While fortunes are liable to change, happiness based on virtue allows one to bear misfortunes in a noble way.

Accordingly, another central concept in Aristotle's ethics is virtue or excellence (*aretē*), in terms of which he spells out what a happy life consists in. Virtues are acquired traits of character that enable one to choose the good, that is, noble, useful and pleasant things and to avoid the bad, that is, shameful, harmful, painful things. Thus, the virtues are important because they make it possible to lead a happy life. However, it isn't very helpful to think of virtuous activity as a means to a happy life, as if the latter was an independently specified goal. Rather a virtuous life is what a happy life consists in. (*See also,* Socrates.) On the other hand, because Aristotle thinks we can be held responsible for our character, we can also be morally judged for whether we posses virtues. Thus, a person may, for example, be blamed for having become someone who doesn't care. Similarly, if a person engages in actions that she knows will make her unjust, she is unjust voluntarily or by choice, even though it doesn't follow that she can stop if she wishes. In line with this (and presumably under the influence of Socrates), Aristotle maintains that acting unjustly is worse than suffering injustice. For although suffering injustice may reduce one's happiness, doing injustice is both wrong towards others and implies a vice. An unjust person isn't only guilty for causing suffering to others, but also for living her life in a way that will not allow her to attain happiness.

As these points illustrate, virtues are practised both in relation to oneself and to others. According to Aristotle, the worst kind of people are those who act viciously in relation to themselves and others, and the best are those who act virtuously in both respects. However, although we can use virtue concepts to describe the rightness of actions and the goodness of persons, that doesn't fully capture their function in Aristotle. For example, the difference between a cowardly man who performs a certain action despite being scared, and a courageous man who does the same without fear isn't that one of them does what is right and the other fails to do so. Rather, the courageous man differs from the cowardly man in leading a happier or more successful life because his actions and feelings are in harmony, unlike those of the cowardly man.

Aristotle divides virtues into two types. On the one hand, there are the so-called intellectual (or theoretical) virtues, for example, wisdom, judgment and practical wisdom, which pertain to the use of reason. On the other hand, there are the virtues of character, for instance, generosity, temperance, courage, truthfulness, friendliness and justice. These virtues pertain to appetites and desires that can be controlled by reason, though are not completely under its control. While virtues of the intellect are developed through teaching, virtues of character are the result of habituation. To learn good habits early on makes all the difference, Aristotle emphasizes, though it isn't enough to get the right upbringing. One must continue to practise and develop good habits. Generally speaking, virtue, therefore, is acquired through its exercise and the origin and means of the corruption of virtue are the same as those of its development. For example, by performing just actions we become just, that is, we come to love justice and take pleasure in such actions, rather than doing them out of fear or because the law requires them. However, we may similarly become unjust by acting in certain ways.

But in order for an action to qualify as virtuous, it isn't enough for it to possess some quality, such as being just or courageous. That kind of action can also occur by accident or under someone else's guidance. Hence, it can't be merely the external quality, so to speak, of the action that makes it virtuous. In addition, the agent must act from, as Aristotle puts it, a firm and unshakeable character. She must perform the action with knowledge of what she is doing and from rational choice, and the action must be chosen for its own sake.

Aristotle further characterizes the idea of a virtuous action in terms of his so-called theory of the mean. The mean is what lies between the extremes of excess and deficiency, and hitting the mean is what it is to get things right. Virtue is what enables one to attain the mean, while doing things to excess or deficiently constitutes (or indicates) a vice. For example, generosity is between stinginess and wastefulness. (The mean is equidistant from the extremes, but not in the sense of being the same for everyone, but determined relative to the agent.) In this connection virtue means specifically virtue of character because it is in connection with actions and feelings that one can talk about excess, deficiency and the mean. For example, one may feel too little or too much fear or confidence. Too much fear marks a coward, too little a rash person. Too much anger may make one lose one's capacity to think clearly, but one may also get insufficiently angry and, consequently, perhaps risk being be walked over by others. Pleasure and pain generally can be experienced too much or too little. To experience pleasure and pain '[. . .] at the right time, about the right things, towards the right people, for the right end, and in the right way is the mean and the best' (*NE*, 1106b). Accordingly, the mean is about, for instance, feeling things in the right proportion, relative to the situation and fitting to the agent. Similar considerations apply to actions. For example, one may drink and eat too much, too little – or in the right way, as the virtuous person does.

To help us to find the mean Aristotle also provides concrete practical advice. Each of us have natural tendencies and we can find out what they are by the pain and pleasure that we feel in connection with different types of actions. For example, intemperate people find abstaining from pleasures oppressive, but temperate people don't. In order to hit the mean one should then drag oneself in the opposite direction and a bit further than one's natural tendencies suggest. For instance, the stingy should do what they would otherwise tend to regard as wasteful.

Importantly, Aristotle's doctrine of the mean isn't a doctrine about moderation. Aristotle isn't saying, for example, that one should always get only moderately angry, regardless of whether a great injustice or some insignificant thing is at stake. Sometimes it may be right to get extremely angry and anything less would be deficient. Virtue can now be characterized as a state involving rational choice which consists in choosing the mean relative to us as determined by reason. Nevertheless, not every action admits a mean. 'Some have names immediately connected with depravity [. . .]', for example, murder and stealing (*NE*, 1107a). There's no good way of performing such actions. In their case one can never hit the mark, but committing such actions is, without qualification, to miss the mark. Similarly there is no mean in being a coward or unjust. (*See also*, THICK AND THIN MORAL CONCEPTS.) Thus, Aristotle's doctrine of the mean is a way to think about what *right* choice involves. It isn't applicable to all possible actions and choices, but only to those for which there is a right and virtuous way of doing them.

Further reading

Aristotle (2000), *Nicomachean Ethics*, R. Crisp (ed.). Cambridge: Cambridge University Press.

Hughes, G. J. (2001), *Routledge Philosophy Guidebook to Aristotle on Ethics*. London: Routledge.

Rorty, A. O. (ed.) (1980), *Essays on Aristotle's Ethics*. Berkeley and Los Angeles: University of California Press.

Hume, David

Hume (1711–1776) is one of the greatest British moral philosophers. His thought wasn't well received during his lifetime, apparently because of his openly critical attitude towards religion, and presumably also because his ethics is entirely secular. Consequently, Hume was unable to find any position in a university, but acquired his living by other means. He did, however, influence certain moral philosophers of his time, such as the fellow Scots Adam Smith and Thomas Reid, and overall has had a great impact. For instance, he is an important background figure for contemporary non-cognitivism in METAETHICS (see, COGNITIVISM AND NON-COGNITIVISM). According to Hume, rather than to be regarded as the object of true or false statements, morality is more properly felt than judged. He has been read as a proto-utilitarian, and he does, indeed, regard utility as a foundation of virtues such as JUSTICE. Overall, however, the aspirations of his moral philosophy are quite different from those of the utilitarians, and he doesn't seek to establish utility as an overarching moral principle, or the foundation of morality (see, UTILITARIANISM). Hume's two great moral philosophical works are the third book of *A Treatise of Human Nature* (1739–40), the *magnum opus* of his youth, and his later rewrite of this third book under the title *An Enquiry Concerning the Principles of Morals* (1751).

The purpose of Hume's investigations into morality is to find the psychological principles that underlie the institution of morality. More specifically, he sets out to establish the general principles that are the basis of the approbation or inapprobation of certain traits of character, in other words, the grounds for regarding some characteristics as virtues and others as vices. Such character traits, according to Hume, are the ultimate object of moral evaluation; particular actions and motives are merely indications of an agent's virtues or vices. The principles that Hume's enquiries seek to uncover are meant to be universal, not culture specific. He believes that the divergent moral views held at different times and by different cultures, for example, those of the ancient Athenians and the British of his day, are manifestations of the very same underlying principles that find a distinct expression in varying circumstances. Accordingly, Hume sees himself as engaged in a scientific inquiry into human nature, that is, into the mental resources and abilities that are the foundation of moral evaluation and moral action. He envisages his investigation as comparable to Newton's investigation of the principles of inanimate nature.

Rather than to put forward a normative theory of morality, his goal is to provide a naturalistic account of how moral judgment is possible.

According to Hume, the foundation of morality isn't reason, but the passions, such as grief, joy, hope and fear (which are direct and immediate), and love, pride, hate and humility (which are indirect and involve reflection of oneself in relation to others). At bottom, however, all passions are affective responses to pleasure and pain. Rather than by reason, morality is therefore determined by feelings or sentiments, that is, by human beings' emotive responses to actions, character traits, and so on. '[W]hen you pronounce any action or character to be vicious, you mean nothing, but that from the constitution of your nature you have a sentiment or feeling of blame from the contemplation of it.' (*Treatise*, Bk. 3. Ch. 1.1, para. 26) Accordingly, moral value isn't a characteristic of anything in reality as such. Our perception of value is a matter of our reacting in particular ways towards reality. As Hume also explains, moral characteristics are comparable to colours in that they have no existence independently of how they affect the sensible beings who perceive them. They are perceptions of the mind rather than qualities of objects as such.

Hume seeks to support this view of moral value and morality by an argument about the motivational inertness of reason, which also constitutes the core of his rejection of rationalism in ethics. According to him, the task of reason or understanding is merely to establish what is true or false. There is, so to speak, a gap between the cognitive recognition of something as true, and coming to act on this basis. For example, my perception or belief that someone is threatening my life doesn't as such motivate any action, but the action I might take, if any, depends on whether I desire to live, and so on. Given its task or role, reason therefore is able to instruct and influence the passions, but has no motivational force of its own and can't set any goals for action. (Sometimes this conception, still in circulation, is called the 'belief-desire model'.) Reason for Hume is more like an advisor of the passions rather than the ruler of the soul that determines what to do. (By contrast, *see* REPUBLIC. Kant's argument for the possibility of practical reason, and his conception that reason can 'necessitate the will' also run contrary to Hume's conception. *See* KANT and GROUNDWORK.)

On the above grounds Hume rejects the account – dominant in antiquity but with prominent representatives in his time too – that morality is something discovered or deduced by reason, and that a requirement for being moral is one's actions being controlled by reason. In short, accepting as a fact morality's ability to motivate action, Hume infers from reason's motivational inertness that morality can't be discovered by reason. A more specific point he makes in this connection is that an explanation is required to legitimize the move from statements about how things are to statements about how things ought to be. But no such explanation, Hume says, is given by the authors of moral systems known to him. They move inconspicuously from one kind of statement to the other, without any acknowledgement of the involvement of passions, assuming to be able to deduce statements about how things ought to be, or value judgments, from statements of fact.

Importantly, Hume's passion-based account shouldn't be understood as subjectivism, according to which what is morally GOOD or bad is merely a personal matter of preference. In Hume's view, moral judgment-making isn't simply a matter of acting instinctively on one's sentiments or passions. A crucial element of morality is reason's correcting the natural personal sentiments. Morality requires a capacity to separate oneself from one's immediate position, and to understand how things would look from different points of view. It therefore involves the attainment of an objective view point, which Hume spells out as something intersubjective, as involving the comprehension of a variety of different positions that agents might occupy. Ultimately then, the object of a moral sentiment isn't a character trait of any particular person, but the character trait as such, considered abstractly, a universal, not a particular.

Accordingly, morality requires, for example, overcoming the natural partiality of sympathy biased to the benefit of those who are close to one. (See, IMPARTI-ALITY.) On Hume's sentimentalist view, sympathy as an imaginative capacity to understand the passions and sentiments of others, and to undergo experiences similar to theirs, is a key component of the foundation of morality. Sympathy, ultimately, makes possible the comprehension of the others' positions and situations. Nevertheless, acting from immediate sympathy would lead to chaos and conflict of interests. Hence sympathy too requires correction by reason, and morality can't be explained simply by reference to it. (Lacking a distinct qualitative feel of its own, Hume doesn't regard sympathy as a passion. Sympathy, however, makes possible the communication of passions.)

Hume defines virtue as '[W]*hatever mental action or quality gives rise to a spectator the pleasing sentiment of approbation*; and vice the contrary.' (*Enquiry*, Appendix I, para. 11) Thus, something being a virtue or a vice consists in it arousing a certain sentiment or feeling. Morally laudable actions, in turn, are ones that arise from virtuous motives such as a virtuous person possesses, and motives that are traceable back to a person's character are generally the basis of the praise and blame of actions. However, to avoid circularity in the explanation, Hume emphasizes, the notion of a moral motive must be explained independently of our sense of the moral value of an action. That some action would be virtuous can't be the original or ultimate motive for performing it without the explanation becoming circular. Similarly, moral duties must be grounded on passions capable of producing them independently of the sense of duty.

Hume divides virtues into two classes, the natural and the artificial. A virtue is natural insofar as there is an impulse or a passion for it that one possesses by nature, simply by being a normal human being. Artificial virtues, on the other hand, are based on conventions. A central example of the latter is JUSTICE, which Hume explains as arising from considerations of utility in particular conditions of scarcity of resources and the selfish nature of human beings. Without such circumstances of external and human nature there wouldn't be any motive or room for this virtue. Given such circumstances, however, it is beneficial overall, even if not in every individual case, to keep one's selfish impulses under control and to act according to the rules of justice by which we protect ourselves and our property. (According to Hume, the conventionality of the rules of justice also explains their universality and perfect inflexibility, given that natural passions are always subject to variation and couldn't support universal and inflexible rules.) Justice, according to Hume, is therefore motivated by self-interest, even though self-interested goals are pursued here indirectly. (*See also*, JUSTICE, GOD AND RELIGION.) As for a 'sensible knave', who manages to get away with injustice without damage to his reputation, in Hume's view such a person ultimately only succeeds in damaging his character, exchanging the 'invaluable enjoyment of a character' for 'worthless toys and gewgaws'. (*Enquiry* Ch. 9.2, para. 25; *see also*, REPUBLIC.)

Further reading

Baillie, J. (2000), *Hume on Morality*. London: Routledge.
Hume, D. (1998), *An Enquiry concerning the Principles of Morals*, T. L. Beauchamp (ed.). Oxford: Oxford University Press.
—(2000), *A Treatise of Human Nature, Book III, Of Morals*, D. F. Norton and M. J. Norton (eds). Oxford: Oxford University Press.

Kant, Immanuel

In his theoretical philosophy Kant (1724–1804) seeks to overcome the opposition between empiricism and rationalism, regarding reason and sensibility as complementary faculties that together make possible our comprehension of reality. This duality of reason and sensibility is present also in his practical philosophy, Kant's fundamental idea being that reason constitutes the basis of the commands of morality. Morality, however, can constitute commands only for embodied creatures of a world of sense who don't automatically act according to the commands of reason and morality. For a command is something which it is possible not to comply with. Particularly influential in moral philosophy is Kant's idea of the autonomy of moral subjects. Moral norms are not, as he says, heteronomously imposed on us from outside, but self-imposed. This is why such norms can be regarded as binding on us. Kant's most important moral philosophical works are the *Groundwork of the Metaphysics of Morals* and the *Critique of Practical Reason* (1788). (*See*, GROUNDWORK.)

A key characteristic of Kant's ethical thought is his emphasis on the unconditionality of morality and its requirements. The bindingness of the requirements of morality, he insists, isn't conditional, for instance, on one's desire for happiness, or on one's being a beneficent person who wants to do good for others. For if the bindingness of the requirements of morality depended on one's possession of some such contingent characteristic such as beneficence, the demands of morality would be contingent too. Accordingly, although Kant acknowledges it to be a general fact about humans that they desire happiness, were this desire the basis of the demands of morality, these demands would apply to humans generally but not unconditionally or by necessity. However, it is central to Kant's moral philosophy that the laws of morality command us with absolute necessity and apply to everyone without exception, that is, universally.

To account for the unconditionality of the commands of morality we must, according to Kant, regard morality as having an *a priori* foundation that is independent of anything empirical and contingent. This foundation he finds in reason and its capacity to determine our will, whereby reason is taken to be an essential capacity of humans, with rationality understood as the ability to act according to presentations of universal laws. Already on this basis a certain limiting condition can be defined which we ought to observe in our actions simply by virtue of being rational beings. This limiting condition Kant calls the 'basic law of pure practical reason', formulating it in the *Critique of Practical Reason* as follows: 'So act that the maxim of your will could always hold at the same time as a principle of universal legislation.' (§ 7)

This basic law, Kant says, is the basis of all morality. It is the moral law from which all our moral duties can be derived. (He also calls the law 'the supreme principle of morality' and its formula the 'categorical imperative'.) Having been determined without reference to anything external and contingent to our being, the moral law can be understood to govern us by necessity. But it is a law that governs us in the capacity of autonomous beings, not as an external constraint. By reference to the moral law the concepts of GOOD and EVIL can then also be defined as absolute concepts, that is, as not relative to or defined by reference to the empirical concepts of agreeable and disagreeable. Similarly, the concept of the moral worth of an action emerges as an absolute one. The moral value of an action depends entirely on the action being moti-vated by the moral law, in other words, the law being the determining principle of one's will or the maxim on which one acts. (For the notions of a maxim, categorical imperative and Kant's argument for his view of the determination of the moral value of actions, see *GROUNDWORK*.)

Assuming the principle of autonomy of will – that is, that the law governing the will has not been imposed on it from outside – what one ought to do or what one's duties are as defined by the moral law, can be known with abso-lute (apodictic) certainty. On Kant's account, knowing what one's duty is doesn't require one to possess worldly prudence, that is, to understand the workings of the world, unlike knowing how to become happy and remain happy. Similarly, given that only the principle that motivates one's will counts in determining the moral worth of actions, acting according to the require-ments of morality is, in principle, under everyone's command at all times. The possibility of moral action doesn't depend on one's abilities and the favoura-bility of external circumstances, unlike the possibility of leading a happy life.

However, given that humans are not perfectly rational but finite, sensible beings whose wills may, besides reason, be determined by impulses of sensibility and desires, we may fail to be governed in our actions by the moral law. (See, EVIL.) In cases where one's actions are in conformity with the law, although motivated by other impulses, they may still be said to be legally, though not morally right. In such a case only the letter but not the spirit of the moral law is fulfilled. In order for an action to have true moral worth, the agent must act out of respect towards the law, motivated by what the law commands. But here it is important to note that, although Kant assumes the identification of our duties to be straightforward, uncertainty pertains to the motives of our actual actions. Doubts can always be raised as to whether a particular action was motivated by duty, or whether the motive was really a covert impulse of self-love or desire for one's own happiness. Hence, although we as moral agents are independent and self-sufficient in the sense that the possibility of moral action isn't conditioned by the contingencies of the external world (as Kant holds in a manner reminiscent of Stoic ethics), we are not infallible or incapable of self-deception. (See, stoic ethics.)

As regards the place of the concept of happiness in Kant's ethics, by happiness he understands a person's maximum well-being (or consciousness of the agreeableness of life) presently and in the future. Different things, however, may make people happy and one person's conception of happiness can vary over time. Hence, there can be no a priori rules regarding the attainment of happiness that are valid necessarily and universally. This also means that were people to adopt as the guiding principle of their actions the attainment of their own happiness, conflicts would arise between them and their principles, as one person's happiness might not harmonize with that of another. Acting according to this principle would, therefore, Kant argues, abolish morality. Rather than completely abandoning the idea of a happy life, and declaring it to be opposed to morality, however, Kant makes room for it in a different way. According to him, morality doesn't require us to give up the claim to happiness, only to not take it into account, or make it our concern, when duty is at stake. (Virtue is defined as the moral attitude exhibited in the struggle to always act as duty commands.) Nevertheless, attending to one's own happiness is still an indirect duty because happiness or, for example, health and wealth, contain the means to the fulfilment of duty. Correspondingly, the lack of happiness tempts one to transgress duty.

Finally, pertaining to the justification of the moral law as something objectively real, not just an illusion or a subjective idea, according to Kant, no non-circular argument can be given here. (He did attempt such a justification in the GROUNDWORK, but later regards it as unsuccessful.) Rather, our consciousness of the moral law and the necessity by which it commands us is, as Kant puts it, 'a fact of reason'. This is an undeniable fact which is exhibited in people's conduct and thoughts about how they ought to act. Similarly, no argument can be given for the reality of FREEDOM presupposed by the possibility of morality. Freedom is a 'postulate of practical reason' (along with the immortality of soul and the existence of God which Kant takes to be conditions of the attainment of the highest GOOD, the union of moral worthiness and happiness). Such postulates can be neither proved nor disproved theoretically, but we are justified in assuming them, according to Kant, because the possibility of morality requires them. (*See,* GOD AND RELIGION.)

Regarding Kant's heritage, his view that the basis of morality can be found in a single supreme principle has sometimes been interpreted (in analytic philosophy) as the idea that there could be something like a decision procedure in ethics, that is, that ethics can be codified in mechanically applicable rules. It isn't clear that Kant himself took ethics to be codifiable in rules in this strong sense, however. In the *Critique of Pure Reason* he characterizes understanding as a power of rules, that is, an ability to subsume things under rules. There are not, however, any rules to be given for what falls under a particular rule. Any further rules would presumably again require further rules to determine how the other rules are to be applied. In this sense judgment is a talent that can't be taught, he maintains. The power of judgment is a feature of what Kant calls 'mother wit' which is something which one either possesses or one doesn't. Furthermore, it seems that mother wit is required, according to him, in the context of moral deliberation too. As he explains in the GROUNDWORK, 'judgment sharpened by experience' is required for knowing where moral laws apply, as well as knowing how to fulfil the demands of the law efficiently (*Groundwork*, 4: 389). If so, Kant should presumably be taken at his word. His spelling out of the supreme principle of morality 'merely' serves the purpose of clarifying the requirements of morality to us, as he states in the *Groundwork*. But it isn't a mechanical device that can do moral thinking on our behalf, as calculators might calculate for us.

Further reading

Kant, I. (1996), *The Critique of Practical Reason*. Indianapolis: Hackett.
Herman, B. (1993), *The Practice of Moral Judgment*. Cambridge, MA: Harvard
    University Press.

Korsgaard, C. (1996), *Creating the Kingdom of Ends*. Cambridge: Cambridge University Press.

Sullivan, R. (1994), *An Introduction to Kant's Ethics* Cambridge: Cambridge University Press.

Wood, A. (1999), *Kant's Ethical Thought*. Cambridge: Cambridge University Press.

Levinas, Emmanuel

The background of Levinas' (1906–1995) philosophy is the phenomenology of Edmund Husserl and its further development in the work of Martin Heidegger. With his attempt to establish ethics as the first philosophy that underlies the rest of philosophy, however, Levinas moves beyond Heideggerian concerns with the question of being. Levinas is a key representative of French deconstruction along with Jacques Derrida, and largely responsible for giving expression to an ethical dimension in deconstruction. Levinas' two main works are *Totality and Infinity* (1961) and *Otherwise Than Being or Beyond Essence* (1974), whereof the latter is often read as his attempt to restate his position consequent to Derrida's discussion of it in the essay 'Violence and Metaphysics'. What is at issue here is Levinas' struggle with the metaphysical language of philosophy. The difficulty is that what he calls 'the face' and 'the other' – two terms that are central to his philosophy – resist conceptualization and capture in language, and therefore can't be domesticated as part of a philosophical (ontological) system. Rather, as his position might be described, an ethical face-to-face situation with the other underlies language in the capacity of a quasi-transcendental condition of its possibility in a broadly Kantian sense. This means that the face-to-face situation can't be described in language in any straightforward way, or be the object of statements. In this respect the status of this notion is similar to Derrida's famous *'differance'* (related to Levinas' notion of a trace) and also to what Wittgenstein's *Tractatus* designates as that which shows itself in language but language can't state.

Levinas' ethics isn't an attempt to define a system of rules that determine how we ought to act; neither is he concerned to characterize an ideal moral agent on whom we ought to model ourselves. Rather, his philosophy is an inquiry into the nature of the ethical. It is an attempt to rethink the foundation of morality, that is, the basis of a subject's having an ethical relation to others at all. This foundation, according to Levinas, is at the same time also the condition for the possibility of social interaction, human community, communication, language, and the significance of anything in general. Thus, Levinas regards human existence as characterized by an underlying ethical dimension; the mode of being of humans is fundamentally ethical. That, of course, doesn't mean that, according to him, we couldn't act unethically.

Rather, acting unethically is only possible for beings who, so to speak, already exist in the sphere of ethics. Only such a being can fail to act ethically and be held responsible for such actions. (By contrast to humans, animals or inanimate objects can't be subjected to moral blame, for example.)

Although the goal of Levinas' considerations regarding the foundation of morality isn't to justify any particular set of values, his work, nevertheless, does give voice to an ethical demand. Through his discussion of the ethical dimension of human existence he reminds us of, and calls us to acknowledge, an ethical demand placed on us, which we may be tempted to ignore. That Levinas doesn't try to establish any particular set of values, therefore, doesn't mean that he is a relativist, though he might be characterized as a pluralist about values. From his point of view, many practices and policies can be acceptable to a degree, but that degree is dependant on how they answer to the underlying ethical demand constitutive of being human. (*See*, RELATIVISM.)

A key observation behind Levinas' philosophy and ethics is that throughout its history Western philosophy has given primacy to the subject. Everything else is determined in relation to the subject, that is, as an object of its consciousness or as part of its world. This, however, amounts to the non-recognition of otherness in any genuine sense. Otherness escapes thematization in that by conceptualizing and naming it, one thereby fixes and determines it. Thus, a conceptual order (or the order of reason) is imposed on otherness: the other is either tagged as the same as something else or different. In any case, otherness is incorporated into a totality or a system of sameness and difference – a system of relations and determinations. Consequently, what Levinas characterizes as the infinity of otherness is lost. A starting point of his ethical thought, then, is an attempt to articulate what the recognition and acknowledgement of otherness and of another person would involve. The question is: how would respect for the other's subjectivity, singularity, particularity and separateness be possible? An aspect of Levinas' considerations, or their partial motive, is a fear of moralistic resonances in the term 'ethics'. Ethics, as he understands it, is about encountering the other. One way such an encounter can fail is through one being moralistic: by judging the other in terms of some moral standards imposed on him/her. Such standards also readily lend themselves to the inclusion or exclusion of subjects from the sphere of morality, and the exclusion of otherness.

More specifically, Levinas seeks to explain the nature of the ethical with the help of the notion of the face of the other, and by describing a primordial experience of the self's facing the other. A crucial feature of this face-to-face situation is how the presence of the other's face puts into question the spontaneity of the self (in the sense of the spontaneity of Kantian rational subject; *see, GROUNDWORK*). The face of the other contests the subject in its aspiration to reduce all otherness into itself, and in this sense the face makes a claim on the self. This claim constitutes a breach of the self's world, and limits the self's imperialistic tendencies, calling it to respond to the claim made by the other's face. This demand to respond then is, Levinas maintains, the source of my responsibility towards the other. It is an OBLIGATION that hasn't begun in me, he says, but has smuggled itself in. Given that this responsiveness and responsibility towards the other is what fundamentally constitutes ethics for Levinas, he is then in effect rejecting the Kantian idea of morality as the expression of the autonomy of the subject, and instead regarding ethics as heteronomous – though whether this characterization does full justice to Levinas isn't absolutely clear. Perhaps he is better understood as moving beyond the opposition between autonomy and heteronomy.

As for the status of this account, what Levinas provides isn't an empirical description of an everyday encounter. Rather, his account is meant to bring to view certain underlying structural features of subjectivity. Subjectivity, according to him, is constituted in or through the encounter with the other. The subject therefore isn't something isolated and self-standing in that subjectivity involves responsiveness and responsibility towards another, which are its determinative structures. Thus, to be a human and a subject is an inherently social and ethical matter. (*See also*, CARE.) The relation to the other is also constitutive of language and communication in the sense that communication requires a speaker and an interlocutor, presupposing the intelligibility of not just what is being said but also the intelligibility of *saying* something, of relating to another in a particular way. Accordingly, from Levinas' point of view, speaking to another may be seen as an expression and manifestation of the underlying ethical responsiveness and responsibility.

On Levinas' account, moral responsibility is an obligation towards a singular and particular other. The self's encounter with the other is an encounter between a particular self and a particular other. Ethics, therefore, is prior to universalization and the legislation of universal principles; it isn't grounded on reason but precedes it. (*See also*, CARE.) Nevertheless, society involves rules as well as relations between multiple individuals. Levinas therefore also needs to explain this and how the universal arises from the particular. This he does by introducing the notion of a third party. The face-to-face situation doesn't take place in isolation, but there is always a multiplicity of others to whom I too am another. The one who is another to me also has responsibilities towards others. This creates a situation of comparing and measuring responsibilities, giving rise to a need for universal concepts, principles, laws, and so on. These others also limit my responsibility towards any particular other in the sense that I can't be responsible to everyone to the same extent. Responding to one person's needs may mean I can't respond to another persons needs. Thus a complicated network of responsibilities and relations arises which constitutes the society. This social world is the venue of JUSTICE. In the end human life and morality requires both the universal and the particular.

Further reading

Critchley, S. (1999), *The Ethics of Deconstruction: Derrida and Levinas.* Edinburgh: Edinburgh University Press.

Davis, C. (1996), *Levinas: An Introduction.* Cambridge: Polity.

Levinas, E. and Nemo, P. (1998), *Ethics and Infinity: Discussions with Philippe Nemo.* Pittsburgh: Duquesne University Press.

Morgan, M. L. (2007), *Discovering Levinas.* Cambridge: Cambridge University Press.

Nietzsche, Friedrich

Nietzsche (1844–1900) is a radical critic of European morality and moral philosophy who urges an examination of the value of moral values, and calls future philosophers to the task of the creation of new values. A fundamental point of Nietzsche's criticism of modern moral philosophy is that, in their attempts to justify morality as something timeless and universal, or to explain it in psychological terms as based on human nature, philosophers have simply taken as given the extant European moral values. (See KANT, HUME, UTILITARIANISM.) These values, however, are the outcome of a contingent historical process and can't be taken as representative of morality as such. Nietzsche supports his claims by presenting a genealogy, that is, a history of the birth and development of European morality, knowledge of which, he believes, is required for addressing the question of the value of values. A comprehension of this genealogy, he hopes, may also help us find a way forward to a higher morality and humanity yet to be spelled out. With regards to the swift actualization of latter prospect, Nietzsche isn't optimistic. He feels people aren't yet ready to hear his philosophy, and therefore sees himself as writing for the future. Nietzsche's style is often aphoristic, reliant on metaphor, polemic and provocative. He assumes a fair amount from the reader. As a consequence he has been often misunderstood, mispresented, and also exploited for purposes that contradict his own, most (in)famously in support of Nazism. Until recently, Nietzsche has exerted far greater influence on the so-called continental than on analytic philosophy, and is an important background figure for Michel Foucault, for instance. Nietzsche's central moral philosophical works are *Thus Spoke Zarathustra* (1885), *Beyond Good and Evil* (1886), and *On the Genealogy of Morals* (1887).

As for Nietzsche's critique of morality and moral philosophy he maintains that, characteristic of European morality is its regard for IMPARTIALITY and unselfishness as key components of morality. Typically these values are built in into moral philosophical systems too, for instance, Kantian ethics and utilitarianism. Theories are also developed to explain how self-sacrificing behaviour and JUSTICE could arise from human nature which is posited at bottom as selfish. (*See*, HUME, IMPARTIALITY.) In Nietzsche's view, however, moral philosophy of this kind (when sincere) is nothing more than a form of good faith in dominant morality. It merely gives a new expression to the dominant morality, avoiding any questions that problematize it. According to Nietzsche, philosophy thus practised has lost sight of the problems involved in morality, that is, what kind of interests and goals particular moralities incorporate and serve, and therefore what their value is. Such problems we can come to see only by comparing different moralities. More specifically, Nietzsche maintains, the problem with European morality is that it constitutes a denial of life – which in itself is a cruel and violent process of appropriating, injuring, overpowering, incorporating and imposing, characterized by inequalities and hierarchies. The dominant European morality, however, is one of mediocrity, a herd morality which is the same for all and leaves no room for exceptional, higher individuals. Ultimately, with the secularization of Europe, it is in danger of leading to nihilism, the disappearance of all meaning and value from life: belief in and will to nothing.

How Europeans have come to this pass is explained through Nietzsche's genealogy. According to him, the current European morality is the result of a struggle between two different modes of morality which he calls the 'master morality' and the 'slave morality'. In this struggle the latter has ultimately taken the upper hand. The origin of value concepts and distinctions, however, lies with the 'masters', the strong and noble who originally invented the term 'good' to refer to themselves and derivatively to their actions. Aware of their difference from the weak, common and contemptible others, they marked these others by the term 'bad', the distinction between good and bad being an expression of their power. (Accordingly, 'good' doesn't originally mean what is beneficial and useful to others, as the philosophers that Nietzsche calls the 'English psychologists' presume.)

The creation of the master morality is followed by a history during which the overpowered and weak acquire cleverness as a means of survival. It also involves their developing consciousness as an inner outlet for violent instincts that they can't otherwise satisfy. Through such transformations what is later called the 'soul' is created, acquiring depth and breadth in the weak and in a 'priestly type' of noble, although this reflectivity also intensifies suffering by intensifying an individual's awareness of it. Thus the human being becomes, as Nietzsche says, an interesting animal. As part of this process, the weak create their own value concepts and distinctions, the slave morality, whose purpose is, essentially, survival and making life bearable. They coin the term 'evil' to refer to the fear inspiring noble and their actions, contrasting this with 'good' by which they mean something quite different from what the noble originally meant by it. Now good is something unthreatening and harmless. Slave morality, according to Nietzsche, is a morality of utility, and values pity, humility, patience, helpfulness and industriousness. In the course of this history, the notion of happiness as attainable for the weak in another life is also invented, and thus the concept of God, as a kind of coping mechanism. For, as Nietzsche notes, it isn't suffering as such that humans can't bear, but meaningless suffering. The invention of God together with the transformation of the concept of guilt into sin gives meaning to suffering by explaining it. A final chapter in Nietzsche's genealogy is what he calls a 'slave revolt in morality'. This consists in the weak succeeding in getting the powerful to adopt their morality with the help of the priestly type of noble, whose power interests this serves. This last phase, 'the most intelligent revenge' of the weak, full of resentment, begins with Jews and their long history of slavery, continuing in Rome with the Christians, and leading to the re-evaluation of the Greek (or Greco-Roman) values. The strong now come to doubt their entitlement to what was theirs by the right of strength.

Morality for Nietzsche, therefore, is something created rather than discovered. As he also says, there are no moral phenomena, only the moral interpretation of phenomena, that is, interpretations of reality in light of particular moralities. That morality is a human creation, however, doesn't mean that we could adopt just any set of values. Rather, morality serves life and this is what its value depends on. Thus even the slave morality's ascetic ideal of self-denial, and its turn away from this world towards happiness in another world, is ultimately to be seen as a trick to preserve life by enabling the weak to survive.

Nietzsche's conception of morality as part of life and in the service of life is also connected with his criticism of Platonic and Kantian philosophy that both seek to ground morality on something beyond life and the sensible world: on the immutable idea of the good and pure reason, respectively. Driven by the conviction that morality must not be contingent like everything in the world of sense, Plato and Kant, in effect, separate morality from life and this world, making humans as moral beings inhabitants of a different world. The key problem with this for Nietzsche, besides the rejection of life, is that Plato and Kant misleadingly suggest that moral knowledge has an entirely different status from all other knowledge. Knowledge, according to Nietzsche, is always perspectival, informed by particular interests that are part of life. When presented as not being part of life, the moral values, concepts and distinctions gain a wrong appearance of objectivity, as if they were independent of any particular perspectives and not informed by any specific interests. (By contrast, Nietzsche – like Hume – regards objectivity as something that involves the comprehension of many diverse perspectives. See, HUME.) A particular morality is thus presented dogmatically as the only possible morality, the exclusive moral interpretation of the phenomena and *the* moral truth. In this regard Platonic and Kantian philosophy resemble Christianity which, according to Nietzsche, is a 'closed system' in the sense that it doesn't leave any room for alternative interpretations of the phenomena, but presents itself as the exclusive interpretation. Accordingly, Nietzsche argues, in Kant's moral philosophy pure reason and the moral law simply take the place of God. Ultimately, Nietzsche's disagreement with moral philosophers then isn't that the description (systematization, and so on) of the currently dominating morality wouldn't be a worthy task. Rather, his problem is the philosophical systems' claim to exclusive moral truth. Similarly, he doesn't deny the value of slave morality either, but its claim to be the sole moral truth.

In place of philosophers' attempts to establish a particular set of moral values as *the* moral values, Nietzsche proposes a more modest descriptive project of the natural history of morals. (*See also,* NATURALISM AND NON-NATURALISM, NORMATIVE ETHICS.) The task of philosophy thus conceived is to collect material, formulate concepts, bring order into the realm of moral feelings and value distinctions that 'live, grow, reproduce and are destroyed', as well as to attempt to illustrate the more recurring shapes, such as the slave and master morality (*BGE,* §186). Apparently, such a project could, minimally, help us understand more clearly our current moral state. On the background of the complicated history of European morality, modern men and their actions are determined by a diversity of morals. We perform, as Nietzsche puts it, multi-coloured actions that receive their illumination from more than one sun, and different moralities can be found juxtaposed inside one and the same person. However, assuming that Nietzsche's genealogy of morals itself is an example of the relevant kind of a descriptive project, such a philosophy might apparently do more than clarify our current state. For what Nietzsche's account of the development of morality seems to achieve is making the dominant morality seem less inevitable by providing us with a possible alternative way to understand the phenomena of morality. In this sense his account has a liberating effect, and opens a route towards the possibility of the articulation of a new higher morality on the basis of the current one. This would constitute our overcoming of the present humanity and the becoming of what Nietzsche calls the 'overhuman'.

Further reading

Berkowitz, P. (1995), *Nietzsche: The Ethics of an Immoralist*. Cambridge, MA: Harvard University Press.

Hatab, L. J. (2008), *Nietzsche's 'On the Genealogy of Morality': An Introduction*. Cambridge: Cambridge University Press.

Nietzsche, F. (1994), *On the Genealogy of Morality*, K. Ansel-Pearson (ed.). Cambridge: Cambridge University Press.

—(2002), *Beyond Good and Evil*, R-P Horstmann and J. Norman (eds). Cambridge: Cambridge University Press.

Socrates

Socrates (469–399 BC) is for many *the* philosophical hero. Not only did he devote his life to philosophical, in particular, moral examination, choosing poverty over comfort, but he also gave his life for this activity. Socrates was condemned to death by an Athenian court on the accusation of corrupting the youth and serving gods not recognized by the state. Regarding his influence, Socrates' articulation of the idea that happiness, welfare or *eudaimonia*, is the ultimate goal of human life, laid a framework for all subsequent Greek and Greco-Roman moral philosophy. (*See,* NICOMACHEAN ETHICS.) According to this view, *eudaimonia* – by reference to which the notion of a good life is explicated – is the last reason in the chain of reasons we could give for our actions. There are no further reasons for wanting to be happy or lead a good life beyond the desirability of happiness or a good life. Even more influentially, Socrates' method of searching for overarching, universal definitions of concepts has provided a model for most subsequent philosophical inquiry, beginning with Plato and Aristotle. (*See,* METHODOLOGY.) Socrates himself never wrote anything, though he inspired a genre of writing, the Socratic dialogues. Consequently, his thought is only known from secondary sources, the most famous of which are Plato and Xenophon. In the case of Plato, scholars widely share the view that only his earlier dialogues are representative of Socrates' thought, while in the later dialogues the character of Socrates becomes more of a mouthpiece for Plato's own philosophy. (*See,* REPUBLIC.) This is an aspect of the so-called Socratic question, concerning the identity of the man and his thought.

For Socrates the most urgent question is: how should one live one's life? On the basis of the explanation that happiness or welfare, the human GOOD, is the final goal of all action and choice, this question may also be expressed thus: what is a good or happy life? Formulated in this way, the urgency of the question finds its expression in Socrates' insistence that to live one's life well or in the right way is even more important than living at all. In other words, the highest value should be attached, not to living, but to living well. Accordingly, maintains Socrates, we should regard the perfection of our souls as the most important task of our lives: 'I spend all my time going about trying to persuade you [. . .] to make your first and chief concern not for your bodies nor for your possessions, but for the highest welfare of your souls [. . .].' (*Apology*, 30a–b)

Indeed, according to Socrates, an unexamined life without the self-examination required for the soul's welfare isn't worth living at all. In this connection it is also important that this search for perfection really must take the form of *self*-examination. For although he is constantly ready to engage others in discussion and to search with them, he simultaneously denies that he would have any knowledge about these matters that he could impart to others, as if trying to give them what they can only find themselves. (Presumably, Socrates' paradoxically sounding claim to wisdom and yet ignorance is to be understood in this light.) Most famously, Socrates' conviction about the importance of living well is exhibited in his choosing to die rather than to betray his views and principles about good life in order to save his life, as explained in the defence of his trial. On similar grounds he also refused to escape from prison before his execution, turning down help offered by friends. (*See also*, PERFECTIONISM.)

Another radical point that Socrates insists on is that doing injustice is worse than suffering it, that is, that the person who wrongs another damages her own happiness more than that of the other. This is presumably connected with Socrates' emphasis on living well and search for moral perfection. For while I may have no control over, and therefore can't be blamed for, the suffering that others may cause me, I can certainly be blamed for the wrong and injustice I do to others, since my own actions do depend on my choice. Hence, although I may blamelessly suffer wrong, I can't blamelessly incur wrong, and am worse off morally in the latter case. Similarly, Socrates also rejects the idea of the legitimacy of retaliation. Injustice isn't only wrong when I initiate it, but equally wrong in response to an injustice that I have suffered. (*See also*, REPUBLIC, JUSTICE)

According to Socrates, the route to the perfection of soul is the cultivation of virtue, by which he understands character traits such as courage, moderation, justice, piety and wisdom. More specifically, all these forms of virtue, Socrates maintains, are forms of knowledge, and thus virtue, generally, is knowledge. The idea underlying this conception of virtue is that we can desire something bad only if we fail to recognize that it is bad – perhaps due to the complexity of matters, because what certain actions really mean becomes perspicuous only years later, or because we have absorbed mistaken values, assuming that wealth or material pleasures are good, for instance. If we did recognize our object of desire as bad, however, this recognition would free us from the desire to pursue it, Socrates believes. Only a fool would choose a lesser good over the greater good. Thus, for Socrates moral mistakes are intellectual at bottom. Ultimately we do wrong out of ignorance and, therefore, in a certain sense involuntarily, even though we might still be held responsible for our ignorance. More concretely, by pursuing some actual object of my desires I might not be pursuing my intended object of desire, the thing that I really want. For example, by pursuing wealth as the key to happiness, if it's not really such a key, I would be pursuing an object of desire under a mistaken description, somewhat like Oedipus who desired to marry queen Jocasta under an incomplete description that didn't recognize her as his mother. Accordingly, Socrates maintains, intellectual enlightenment isn't only necessary but sufficient for moral reformation. This view of Socrates too, however, has caused great puzzlement among philosophers who have discussed it under the title of the problem of *akrasia*, that is, weakness of will, moral weakness, or incontinence. Couldn't there be someone who, despite her knowledge of what is good, nevertheless chooses the less good, for instance, some immediate pleasures, due to the weakness of her will? If so, how exactly should this person's mistake or failure be described?

Regarding his conception of virtue, Socrates has been interpreted, for example, by J. S. Mill, as a utilitarian. On this interpretation the value of virtue is instrumental, relative to its contribution to a person's happiness or welfare. Understood in this way, welfare then also needs to be characterized independently of the notion of virtue. For example, it might be defined as pleasure. It seems more plausible, however, to understand Socrates as maintaining that virtue is constitutive of happiness, that is, a necessary and a sufficient ingredient of happiness, not a means to an independently specified goal. According to this view, in order for someone to be happy, they must possess virtue, and indeed virtue alone is sufficient for happiness. However, unlike the Stoics' position, this need not be taken to imply that everything else besides virtue would be indifferent, of no importance for happiness. (*See*, STOIC ETHICS.) Rather than holding that virtue is identical with happiness, and hence that, for instance, the success or failure of one's life projects should make no difference to a virtuous person's happiness, the Socratic view might be understood as follows. Happiness comes in degrees; various things in life can contribute to it. Virtue, however, is the necessary foundation of happiness in the sense that, in order for things such as wealth to contribute to happiness rather than its opposite, virtue is required. Without virtue other things are no good and may become the source of EVIL. On the other hand, given that virtue itself is already sufficient for happiness, a person who possesses virtue will be happy. Thus, there is a sense in which such a person can't be harmed, and is in possession of the highest good. Not that bad things couldn't come her way, and make her life less happy than it would be in some more favourable circumstances. Nevertheless, her most important possession, her virtue, can't be violated. Therefore her happiness too is ultimately inviolable, even if not entirely independent of fortune.

Further reading

Irwin, T. I. (1995), *Plato's Ethics*. Oxford: Oxford University Press.
Plato (1961), *Apology, Gorgias, Protagoras,* in Hamilton, E. and Cairns, H. (eds.), *The Collected Dialogues of Plato*. Princeton: Princeton University Press.
Vlastos, G. (1991), *Socrates: Ironist and Moral Philosopher*. Cambridge: Cambridge University Press.

The Key Texts

Aristotle, *Nicomachean Ethics*

Nicomachean Ethics is the most important source on Aristotle's views on ethics (besides the less well-known *Eudemian Ethics*). The book is composed out of Aristotle's notes for lectures he delivered to young upper class Athenian men, expected to take up important positions in the city state. Aristotle emphasizes that the lectures are not simply meant to satisfy a theoretical interest but to have a practical purpose: '[I]t is not in order to acquire knowledge that we are considering what virtue is, but to become good people – otherwise there would be no point in it' (*NE*, 1103b).

As this quote also illustrates, the notion of virtue, which occupies a central place in Aristotle's discussion (*see*, ARISTOTLE), ultimately owes its centrality to the idea that it is in terms of this notion that we can understand what it would be to become and be a GOOD person and what it is to act in the right way. What Aristotle is more fundamentally concerned to grasp in his inquiry is the concept of the highest and most complete good, by which he means the highest and most complete good for human beings. The highest good is something chosen for its own sake, not for the sake of anything else, and it is that for the sake of which everything else is chosen (*See also*, GOOD.).

Aristotle identifies happiness or well-being (*eudaimonia*) as this highest good. (*See*, ARISTOTLE for discussion of the term '*eudaimonia*'.) Happiness is that which we desire for itself and never for the sake of anything else, and it is something for the sake of which the rest of our actions are undertaken. Happiness, Aristotle explains, means living well and acting well. This is important because, although people generally agree on the identification of the highest good with happiness, and in this sense agree on the concept of the good, they differ in their respective conceptions of happiness. What Aristotle calls the 'masses', for example, confuse happiness with pleasure or wealth.

Often one person may also give different accounts of happiness at different times: when ill, it is health, when poor, it is wealth. More specifically, Aristotle maintains, what happiness or the human good is, can be comprehended by grasping more clearly what the characteristic activity or function of a human being is, that is, the activity or the kind of life distinctive to humans among living beings. For what can be considered doing well for a particular type of being depends on precisely what sort of being it is.

In this sense, Aristotle's account of the highest human good then involves as part of it a conception of human nature. This is a view of human life as life according to reason or intellect which, Aristotle maintains, is the characteristic feature or activity of human beings, in contrast to (other) animals. Moreover, he infers, given that the use of reason is an activity of the soul rather than of the body, and that the characteristic activity is accomplished well when it's accomplished according to whatever is a virtuous way doing it, we can say that the human good or happiness is an activity of the soul in accord with virtue. However, what exactly this characteristic activity, and therefore a happy life, consists in is a contested point among Aristotle's interpreters. According to the so-called dominant interpretation, this activity can be identified as contemplation, this being the highest activity a human being can engage in and therefore also the source of the greatest and most complete happiness. According to the so-called inclusive interpretation, the happy life is a package of activities, each desired for its own sake.

Leaving aside this dispute, it is an important feature of Aristotle's view that, according to him, there is no perspective external to a virtuous life from which we can grasp the good. In other words, in order to gain an undistorted view of the good we ourselves must become good. In this sense, to merely possess knowledge of virtue isn't enough but we must also try to attain and exercise it, and it is this point that explains Aristotle's emphasis on the practical aim of his lectures mentioned earlier. This view is also connected with his doubts about the effectiveness of arguments in the area of ethics. As he points out, if arguments were enough to make people good, this would already have been achieved. But arguments seem unable to influence the 'masses' and those who don't already love what is noble. In order for arguments and teaching to be effective, the soul of the recipient must first be prepared through the development of the right kind of habits.

More specifically central to happiness is the development of what Aristotle calls 'practical wisdom' (*phronēsis*), which involves the comprehension of what makes human beings happy and which acts are just, noble and good for a human being. A practically wise person knows what is good for himself and good for people in general, and living in the manner of the practically wise constitutes a happy life. Unlike wisdom or scientific knowledge (*sophia*), practical wisdom can't be identified with knowledge of universal principles (unlike Plato perhaps maintained; *see*, REPUBLIC). Rather, because action and choice concern particulars, practical wisdom requires knowledge of those particulars and how to apply principles in relevant cases. Because it is concerned with particulars, practical wisdom is akin to perception, and because concerned with changing things, akin to judgment. Unlike judgment, however, practical wisdom commands, not merely judges. Notably, because knowledge of particulars is developed partly through experience, young people can't be practically wise. For the same reason, Aristotle says, we ought to attend to the undemonstrated words and beliefs of experienced and older people, or of the practically wise, not just to demonstrations. Their experienced eye enables them to see correctly.

Practical wisdom comes in a package with the virtues of character. (For the virtues of character, *see* ARISTOTLE.) One can't be practically wise without being good in the sense of possessing virtues of character, though one can, for instance, know geometry and not also be good. As Aristotle explains the relation between virtues of character and practical wisdom, virtue makes the aim right, practical wisdom makes it possible to reach the aim in a right way. Although it is possible, in a certain sense, to possess some virtues without possessing them all (e.g. be naturally courageous or prone to temperance), it isn't possible to be good without possessing all the virtues, according to Aristotle. In this sense virtues constitute a unity. To possess practical wisdom is to possess all the virtues, and virtues culminate in practical wisdom.

Beyond the issues mentioned here, the topics discussed in this rich book include, for example, the Socratic problem of the weakness of will. Aristotle also offers detailed discussions of particular virtues, including a discussion of JUSTICE. (*See*, JUSTICE.) The *Nicomachean Ethics* concludes with a lengthy discussion of friendship which Aristotle regards as an important constituent of happiness. This discussion includes, for example, analyses of different types of friendships.

Further reading

Aristotle (2000), *Nicomachean Ethics*, R. Crisp (ed.). Cambridge: Cambridge
   University Press.
Kraut, R. (ed.) (2006), *The Blackwell Guide to Aristotle's* Nicomachean Ethics.
   Oxford: Blackwell.

Immanuel Kant, *The Groundwork of the Metaphysics of Morals*

The task Kant sets himself in the *Groundwork* is to lay a foundation for a pure moral philosophy. By such a philosophy he means one whose key concepts are not derived from experience. More specifically, he seeks to achieve this goal by clarifying and establishing what he calls the 'supreme principle of morality'. Central to Kant's view is that this principle, which lies at the bottom of morality and from which all more specific moral principles can be derived, isn't to be understood as an external constraint to human conduct. Rather, it is a law which human beings issue for themselves, assuming nothing but that they are rational beings. Among Kant's moral philosophical works the *Groundwork* is chronologically first, published in 1785. It is followed by the *Critique of Practical Reason*, similarly concerned with foundational issues (*see*, KANT), and later by the *Metaphysics of Morals* (1797) which discusses at a more concrete level various moral concepts and principles and their role in human life.

As Kant explains, the *Groundwork* isn't meant to inform us about something we didn't know, as if we weren't already able to distinguish right from wrong. Rather, his purpose is to explicate and clarify the concept of morality, through an analysis of common, ordinary moral understanding, in particular the notion of a moral OBLIGATION or duty. Philosophical clarification is required because our understanding may get corrupted and we may be misled, for example, by bad philosophy. Having set out clearly the relevant concepts, Kant then seeks to explain (in the final chapter of the book) the possibility of morality, that is, why we must regard moral principles as binding. This is to show that there really are moral obligations or duties, in other words, that the relevant concepts are not merely empty and illusory (as, for example, the concept of fate might be).

Kant begins his clarificatory undertaking by discussing the concept of a good will. Good will, he argues, is the only thing that is good in itself, absolutely, independently of its relation to anything else. In this sense it has unconditional worth. By contrast, although talents of mind, such as judgment and understanding, and qualities of temperament, such as courage and resolution, are good in many respects, they may also be the basis of EVIL and harm – unless guided by good will. Good will then seems to be the condition of the goodness of actions because only the good will produces good actions by necessity. Accordingly, by coming to understand the principles according to which the good will works, Kant maintains, we can come to comprehend what makes actions morally good.

More specifically, Kant seeks to explicate the concept of good will by focusing on actions done from duty, which exemplify actions from good will. Characteristic of such an action is that it is done for its own sake, or simply out of duty. In this sense the action is an end in itself. It isn't done because it is a condition or a means for achieving something else. Being done simply because it is a duty, an action from duty exhibits the kind of unconditionality that marks moral obligation. Here the agent's motive for action is, as Kant puts it, respect for the moral law and nothing else.

The motive of an action is important because Kant, so it seems, takes the motive to determine the identity of an action. It determines what action doing such and such really constitutes, and consequently also the action's moral worth. For example, a merchant who refrains from deceiving his customers because it is bad for business wouldn't be acting out of respect for the moral law but out of self-interest. Consequently, the conformity of his action with the moral law is merely accidental. The same goes for a beneficent person who helps others because it makes her happy. The maxim, that is, the subjective principle that determines her will and guides her action, differs from that of a dutiful person who helps others because morality requires it. Again, because it is, according to Kant, contingent what makes a person happy, the correspondence of the beneficent action with what is morally right is coincidental and the action can't be attributed unconditional worth. This is also why, Kant argues, the consequences of actions are not what determines their moral value: whatever an action achieves could be brought about by mere accident. Unconditional worth can only be attributed to a will governed or determined by the moral law. (On the other hand, Kant's emphasis on the motive of action as a way to identify the action's nature and moral worth raises the question whether the identity of an action can always be determined independently of its consequences.)

As for the possible principles that can determine a person's will or motivate actions, according to Kant, to be rational is to act on the basis of presentations of universal laws. It is characteristic of a rational being that reason can make its will to obey such laws. A presentation of a universal law that determines or necessitates the will Kant calls a 'command'. Its formula, in turn, is an 'imperative'. Kant identifies two (exclusive) types of imperatives: hypothetical and categorical. A hypothetical imperative (one that commands hypothetically) presents something as a means to a further end. Thus its power of necessitation is conditional to an agent's having an interest in achieving this end. A categorical imperative, by contrast, commands unconditionally, that is, presents an action according to a law as necessary in itself and as universally necessary, without reference to any other end to which its command is conditional. Clearly, to be attributed with unconditional worth the good will and actions emanating from it must be determined by the categorical rather than the hypothetical imperative, given the conditionality of the value of actions motivated by the latter. Accordingly, Kant characterizes the categorical imperative as the 'moral imperative' simply on the basis of its unconditionality, even prior to specifying in the *Groundwork* what exactly it commands.

To specify the categorical imperative and the principle of the good will we must, according to Kant, isolate the will from anything external, that is, from all content and external ends, that might determine it. The will must be characterized solely by reference to its form, which he identifies as nothing but the will's conformity with universal laws, or as the lawlikeness of the will's functioning. The categorical imperative (the supreme principle of morality) then reads: '*I ought never to act except in such a way that I could also will that my maxim should become a universal law*' (*Groundwork*, 4: 402). According to Kant, all imperatives of duty can be derived from this principle, which constitutes a criterion for the permissibility of actions. For example the maxim of making a false promise in order to borrow money would not pass the test of universalization, as the agent would be at the same time both relying on the institution of promising and making an exception for herself from its basic rule that promises must be kept, thus undermining the very institution she is making use of. More generally, breaking the imperative, Kant says, leads to a contradiction: such maxims for actions can't be willed or sometimes even coherently entertained. (*See also*, UNIVERSALIZABILITY.)

In addition to the above basic formula of the law, Kant gives three variant formulations which he says, are equivalent, and apparently meant to highlight different dimensions of the principle and further clarify what acting according to it means. They command (1) to always act according to principles that could be regarded as universal laws of nature, (2) to always treat humanity as an end, not merely a means, and (3) to regard the will of every rational being as autonomous and giving a universal law. The relations between these formulas continue to be discussed by Kant scholars.

As regards the bindingness of the moral law, a hypothetical imperative binds anyone who has a particular end or goal. One can't will an end, but not also the necessary means to it, without compromising one's rationality. The bindingness of the categorical imperative, however, isn't based on the will's relation to anything else, such as an end or an external authority. Rather, it is binding in the capacity of a law that a rational will autonomously issues for itself and whose authors are we as rational beings. We bind ourselves to this law simply by being rational beings, because to be rational is to be bound by this law.

An important presupposition of Kant's conception of morality, therefore, is that humans, as autonomous beings who give a law to themselves, have a free will. The *Groundwork* seeks to support this assumption in its final chapter by arguing that as rational beings we must regard ourselves as free, not merely as belonging to a world of sense determined by causal laws. Reason is spontaneous in the sense that its ideas are not determined by what is given to us through senses but go beyond it. In this sense we are also members of what Kant calls a 'world of intelligence'. We are thus independent of the world of sense and free.

Finally, this conception of humans as belonging, so to speak, to two different worlds, or there being two dimensions to their existence, is also important for Kant's theory of morality in that, as sensuous beings, humans are not simply and perfectly rational. There is a gap between the maxims on which we actually act and the principles of reason: we are subject to inclinations and impulses that may run contrary to morality. (*See,* EVIL.) This is why Kant's theory of practical reason takes the form of a theory of how reason necessitates the will. It is a theory of imperatives, of what we ought to do. For us the moral law states what we ought to do rather than simply describing what we do. (*See,* KANT.)

Further reading

Kant, I. (1998), *The Groundwork of the Metaphysics of Morals*, M. Gregor (ed.). Cambridge: Cambridge University Press.
Timmermann, J. (2007), *Kant's Groundwork of the Metaphysics of Morals: A Commentary*. Cambridge: Cambridge University Press.

John Stuart Mill, *Utilitarianism*

Utilitarianism (1861) is a classic articulation and defence of the utilitarian ethical theory, originally formulated by Jeremy Bentham. In *Utilitarianism* Mill presents some key arguments for the utilitarian moral theory and responds to problems raised by its critics.

According to *Utilitarianism*, the foundation of morality – that what must be determined first in order for us to have clear comprehension of what morality requires from us – is the utility-principle. This principle is the fundamental law at the root of morality and the standard of morality. Mill formulates the principle as follows: '[. . .] actions are right in proportion as they tend to promote happiness, wrong as they tend to promote the reverse of happiness. By happiness is intended pleasure, and the absence of pain; by unhappiness pain, and the privation of pleasure' (*Utilitarianism*, chapter 2, para. 2). Thus Mill designates the tendency of actions to promote happiness as the criterion or test for their rightness or wrongness. The moral worth of actions, in other words, is to be determined, and their justification decided, on the basis of their tendency to promote happiness. Indeed, according to Mill, whatever steadiness and consistency there is in the moral beliefs of humankind, it has mostly been due to the tacit influence of this standard, not explicitly recognized nor properly spelled out before the utilitarian theory. In this capacity, he maintains, the principle of utility has shaped the moral doctrines of even those who wish to reject its authority.

Given the view that the moral value of actions is ultimately determined through the utility-principle, establishing and justifying the principle emerges as *the* central task of moral philosophy for Mill. To establish this principle is to show that all questions of moral evaluation are explainable as questions concerning the promotion of happiness, or as one might put it, that they can all be reformulated as questions of the latter type. More specifically, given Mill's hedonistic account of happiness in terms of pleasure and the absence of pain, this task assumes the form of providing an account of all questions of moral evaluation as questions about the promotion of pleasure or minimization of pain. Accordingly, Mill is required to demonstrate that pleasure is the sole, ultimate GOOD and the only thing desirable as an end.

As regards this demonstration, explains Mill, questions of ultimate ends – or statements of first principles and premises more generally – don't allow for a proof in the normal sense of inferring a conclusion from true premises. Rather, to establish such a principle or premise, one must appeal directly to the faculties by which we judge facts. The only way to prove that nothing is desirable but happiness, and that it is the sole end of human action, is to demonstrate that it is an empirical, psychological fact about human beings that they desire nothing but happiness or what constitutes a part of happiness. Or as Mill also explains, the idea of this demonstration, the proof for something being desirable, is that people actually desire it. Desiring a thing and finding it pleasurable, on the other hand, he maintains, are the same thing. If so, to show that people desire nothing but happiness is also to show that pleasure constitutes the sole good and the ultimate end of action. All desirable things are either desirable for the pleasure inherent in them or desirable as means to pleasure. Anything else, for example, JUSTICE, virtue or the cultivation of virtuous character is only good as a means to pleasure and happiness. (In his critique of naturalistic ethics in PRINCIPIA ETHICA Moore takes Mill's proof as one of his main targets, and aims to show that it involves what he calls the 'naturalistic fallacy'. *See*, PRINCIPIA ETHICA.)

Given the way in which *Utilitarianism* seeks to lay down the foundation for the utilitarian theory, this theory also requires that it is possible to compare the extent to which various courses of action contribute to happiness. In the end this is, for Mill, a matter of comparing pleasures, or how pleasures and pains are balanced in some particular case as opposed to another. (Whereas Bentham only assumed instances of pleasure to be comparable with respect to their quantity, Mill maintains that the quality of pleasure must also be taken into account in making such comparisons. As he famously says, it is better to be a dissatisfied Socrates than a satisfied fool.) On the issue of how such comparisons are to be decided, Mill takes again an empiricist stance. Of two pleasures the more pleasurable is that which all or most of competent judges actually desire. But of the question of how exactly competent judges might be identified without begging questions and bringing in value concepts, *Utilitarianism* says nothing.

In order to avoid misunderstanding, the conception of what it is to be engaged in moral thinking, articulated in *Utilitarianism*, isn't that one should be constantly making pleasure-comparisons. Such comparisons are only the ultimate justificatory ground of moral evaluations. Hence, rather than always having to calculate which action would maximize happiness (maximize pleasure and minimize pain), we may typically let the well established and tested secondary principles of common-sense morality be our guide. In actual moral thinking the utility-principle only plays a role when it comes to questions about the justification of customary practices and principles, or when secondary principles need to be weighed against each other; for instance, when we need to decide whether it might be acceptable to break the rule that forbids lying in some particular case. (Lying, Mill maintains, in opposition to Kant, may sometimes be our moral duty.) Correspondingly, Mill argues that the principles of justice, for example, are explainable and justifiable in terms of the utility-principle. (*See*, JUSTICE.) In this sense the utility-principle is *the* fundamental, but not the only, principle we should have. The secondary principles give content to this fundamental principle and, as Mill explains, it is only the secondary principles that give specific content to a person's moral outlook.

Further reading

Crisp, R. (1997), *Mill on Utilitarianism*. London: Routledge.
Mill, J. S., (1998), *Utilitarianism*, R. Crisp (ed.). Oxford: Blackwell.
West, H. (ed.) (2006), *The Blackwell Guide to Mill's* Utilitarianism. Oxford: Blackwell.

G. E. Moore, *Principia Ethica*

First published in 1903, *Principia* is best known for its notion of a naturalistic fallacy and the so-called Open Question Argument designed to expose this fallacy. Moore's argument delivered a severe blow to naturalism in ethics and has since become a staple topic in textbooks on METAETHICS (*See,* METAETHICS, NATURALISM AND NON-NATURALISM). Although it is part of *Principia's* conception of the GOOD that the goodness of intrinsically good things is universal and objective, this part of Moore's account was abandoned by the so-called non-cognitivists in ethics who came to dominate analytical moral philosophy in Moore's wake, building on his argument against naturalism. (*See,* COGNITIVISM AND NON-COGNITIVISM.)

Moore's central concern in *Principia* is to articulate a theory of value. The motive for this undertaking is his conviction that moral philosophical discussion is permeated by certain fundamental confusions. According to Moore, philosophers have failed to distinguish between different types of questions regarding the good that can be expressed by the ambiguous string of words 'What is good?': (1) What is good as such, or what do we mean by 'good'? (2) What things are good in themselves or intrinsically good? (3) By what means is good brought about, that is, what things are good as means, and what ought we to do? In Moore's view, the first question, which he regards as the most fundamental question of ethics, must be answered before addressing the second and third questions. Before we answer it, we can't know what counts as evidence for any ethical judgment. But even when the first question has been answered, a failure to distinguish between the second and third question makes us unable to judge reliably the truth of assertions about what things are good.

As regards the first question, Moore's answer is that the word 'good' refers to a property, common to all good conduct as well as other good things, which isn't analysable (or definable) in either natural or metaphysical terms. Thus, value judgments constitute a class of their own, not reducible to statements about reality. Natural terms are identified in *Principia* with terms employed by the natural sciences, including psychology – though, in the preface to the second edition, Moore admits this identification to be problematic. While good, according to Moore, is a property of natural objects, it's not a natural property that can be the object of senses. *Pace* naturalism, one can't substitute for good a property of natural objects. Although good things exist in time and are part of nature, goodness itself doesn't have this kind of existence. Moore uses the term 'metaphysical' in opposition to 'natural', crediting metaphysicians with the recognition that not everything that is, is a natural object or quality. Problematically, however, according to Moore, metaphysicians have interpreted assertions about good as concerning a supersensible reality and tried to base ethics on truths about supersensible entities, that is, to infer what is good from claims concerning supersensible reality.

More specifically, attempts to define good in natural or metaphysical terms involve the naturalistic fallacy. (The name for the fallacy is therefore only partly fitting.) Examples from naturalistic ethics are attempts to define something being good as it being pleasurable or desirable, and to identify goodness with pleasure or as what is desired. Moore's target of criticism here is Mill on the one hand, and the evolutionary ethics of Herbert Spencer on the other. (*See*, UTILITARIANISM.) An example from metaphysical ethics is Kant's definition of good as what the moral law commands. (*See* Kant and GROUNDWORK.) According to Moore, such identity claims are problematic, because it is always possible to ask, for example, of pleasure or of what we desire, whether it is actually good. Similarly, one might ask about the moral law whether what it commands is good. That such questions are meaningful shows the identity claims to be non-tautologous, and that the suggested identities are not simply part of the meaning of 'good'. In this sense, Moore maintains, it is always an open question whether anything natural, or supernatural, is good. The open question argument then is the argument about the significance or meaningfulness of such questions.

As regards the notion of intrinsic good, what is intrinsically good or good in itself, Moore explains, is worth having purely for its own sake, not merely as a means to something. According to him, statements to the effect that something is intrinsically good, if true, are universally true. As the method by which it is decided what things are intrinsically good, Moore proposes the method of considering which things, if they existed in themselves or in absolute isolation, would still be good. This allows one to distinguish intrinsically good things from what are merely means to good. More specifically, statements about good as means, Moore asserts, concern causal relations. Because, for example, an action performed in different circumstances will produce different effects, statements about good as means can at most be generalizations (in contrast to universal claims). (*See*, UNIVERSALIZABILITY.)

As the most valuable intrinsically good things, Moore identifies 'certain states of consciousness, which may be roughly described as the pleasures of human intercourse and the enjoyment of beautiful objects' (*PE*, 237). Although he thus clearly regards pleasures of a certain kind as good, he isn't claiming that they are the same as the good as such (or goodness). The latter assertion would involve the naturalistic fallacy. Rather than being put forward as a definition of good, Moore's statement identifies certain things as intrinsically good on the basis of certain natural characteristics they possess. (His statement is synthetic, as all statements about good according to him are, not analytic.) By contrast, virtues and doing what is right or one's duty, Moore considers only as means to good. (Thus, he agrees with Kant about the moral significance of virtues, while being in a fundamental disagreement with Kant about the notions of right and duty. *See*, KANT, GROUNDWORK, VIRTUE ETHICS.) In Moore's view, the proposition 'I'm morally bound to perform this action' is identical with 'This action will produce the greatest possible amount of good'. Similarly, right simply means 'the cause of a good result', which is identical with useful. Accordingly, moral laws, in his view, are merely statements that certain kinds of action will have good effects.

As Moore's view of moral OBLIGATION illustrates, his ethical outlook, beyond his theory of value, is utilitarian or consequentialist. To ask what one ought to do is to ask what kind of effects a particular way of acting would produce. Rather than arguing for this view, however, Moore seems simply to assume that in moral life we should aim for the maximization of the good. The *Principia* does include, however, discussion of some difficulties relating to utilitarianism, and in particular, to the implications of the fact that human beings, as finite beings, are unable to know all the consequences their actions. This is so, Moore holds, because our causal knowledge is incomplete. From this he concludes that we don't actually know what our duties are. All we can know is what kinds of actions generally tend to have good consequences. This is then the way we ought to act, without ever allowing ourselves to deviate in any particular case from rules or laws based on such generalizations. Thus Moore is a rigorist about ethical rules, and his view is open to the charge of so-called rule-worship. (*See*, CONSEQUENTIALISM.)

Further reading

Baldwin, T. (1990), *G. E. Moore*. London: Routledge.

Hutchinson, B. (2001), *G. E. Moore's Ethical Theory: Resistance and Reconciliation*. Cambridge: Cambridge University Press.

Moore, G. E. (1993), *Principia Ethica* (revised edn), T Baldwin (ed.). Cambridge: Cambridge University Press.

Nuccetelli, S. and Seay, G. (eds) (2007), *Themes from G. E. Moore: New Essays in Epistemology and Ethics*. Oxford: Oxford University Press.

Plato, *Republic*

The *Republic* is the most famous of Plato's (472–347 BC) works, and has had great impact on both moral and political philosophy. Its central topic is JUSTICE, that is, what justice is, why one should be just and what the benefits of justice are. Plato's term normally translated as 'justice' is *dikaiosunē* which might also be translated as 'righteousness', indicating the broader meaning of the Greek term. In order to explain the questions addressed in the dialogue and Plato's line of argument, I'll begin by describing the setup of the discussion. (*See also*, JUSTICE.)

The discussion starts from a claim by the sophist Thrasymachus that it is more beneficial for a person to be unjust than just. This claim Socrates, the main figure of the dialogue, seeks to refute, holding the opposite view. Socrates' refutation, however, doesn't satisfy the participants in the discussion. He is requested to clarify his view in more detail, and the question now becomes: Is it better to be just than unjust, even when not recognized as such and unable to reap the benefits of a good reputation? How is being just better than being unjust, when one is able to pass oneself as just and to enjoy the benefits of a good reputation as well as the gains of injustice? To answer these questions a proper understanding of justice is required which Socrates sets out to articulate. In so doing he relies on the assumption that justice is the same thing in the case of a just person and a just city or state, and that what it is to be a just person can therefore be elucidated by clarifying what a just state is like. For, claims Socrates, it is easier to comprehend what justice is when we see it in the larger scale of a city or state. Consequently, as part of his discussion Plato develops a model for an ideal, just city-state, arguing that philosophers should rule it (analogously to the role of reason in an individual) because only they have knowledge of the unchanging forms of things, that is, of the real nature of things. Here is also where Plato presents his famous cave allegory to explain what true philosophical knowledge is in distinction from everyday beliefs concerning contingent empirical reality. (But *see also*, NIETZSCHE.)

Plato's fundamental idea is that justice isn't merely an external characteristic, so to speak, of actions and how one behaves toward others. To qualify as a just person, it isn't enough to act lawfully, giving each their due, and to comply with the rules of justice. That doesn't reach the heart of the matter, and isn't very satisfactory either morally or philosophically. The moral problem here is that it invites a complacent attitude, suggesting that it is sufficient for justice to act as the rules of morality demand, with no self-examination or hard questions required. Moreover, if this is all there is to justice, why not act unjustly for gain, when possible to do so undetected or in a position of power? The view also runs the risk of leading to relativism and consequently scepticism about morality, insofar as the rules of justice are regarded as conventional (although these are not terms Plato uses). For, if justice is merely a convention, why doesn't relativism about justice or morality generally follow? (*See,* RELATIVISM.) And if relativism does follow, why shouldn't we regard justice or morality as just another archaic custom to be abandoned as impracticable? Instead, Plato argues, being just is a particular state of the agent's soul, or of a city, and a virtue of its possessor. At the core of his response to the challenge of why be just then is the claim that not to possess this virtue is damaging to one's life; it prevents one from attaining true happiness, welfare and a good life. But now the question remains, in what way exactly is the possession of the virtue of justice a requirement for a good life? This is what we are supposed to come to understand when we understand the nature of justice, and that, Plato maintains, will make obvious its desirability.

Justice, Plato argues, is desirable both in itself (for its own sake) and because of its consequences (for its effects or rewards). Thus his view is neither consequentialist nor deontological, and justice shouldn't, for instance, be understood as a condition of a good life merely in the sense of a means. (*See,* CONSEQUENTIALISM and DEONTOLOGICAL ETHICS.) For example, justice isn't a kind of necessary compromise with others, as many according to Plato suppose, whereby we agree to forego some of our desires so as to gain in peace and safety as a consequence. Rather, Plato compares justice to health of the body, which is valuable both for its consequences and in itself. Justice, in other words, is a certain kind of a state of well-being of the agent's soul (*psuchē*), or of the city. It is a state in which the different parts of the soul – reason, the desiring or appetitive part, and spirit or passion – or the different classes in the city-state – the philosopher-warrior-guardians, the merchants and the workers – are in harmony. Harmony means here that each part or class performs its own function in accordance with its own nature and specialization, each 'doing its own'. Thus, the soul or city constitutes an integrated well functioning unity.

More specifically, Plato develops his account of the just city and the city-soul-comparison as follows. Just as it is the proper function of reason to control desires, so it is the proper function of the philosopher-guardians (who are men and women alike) to rule the state. For this task the city provides the guardians with a long and rigorous character forming education. The ultimate focus of their study is Goodness itself, the Form of which provides the conceptual standard against which all ordinary good things are judged good. As a result, the guardians become wise and selfless; they are completely devoted to the happiness of the city as a whole, not their own interests, and thus impartial. (*See also*, IMPARTIALITY.) A city ruled thus by the best – by an elite whose superior knowledge leaves no room for moral disagreements – becomes wise through the wisdom of the guardians. Similarly, a soul controlled by reason and guided by knowledge rather than by desire or passion will thrive – although passion still has an important role, motivating the person, backing up reason and making our desires amenable to reason.

Thus Plato understands by justice in the individual essentially a kind of psychic harmony, which he takes to be necessary for flourishing and living a good life. Part of this account is that justice requires knowledge, that is, that our lives are guided by a comprehension of how things really are. This account of justice as psychic harmony is meant then, ultimately, to explain the value and desirability of the virtue of justice for an individual. Interestingly, it is an agent-centred account that construes justice as a state of the agent along virtue-ethical lines, though not an account of justice where principles play no role, insofar as knowledge of the essence of things or forms is to be taken to involve in some sense the grasp of universal principles. Given these general characteristics of Plato's account, however, various questions remain open about exactly how his conception of justice is to be understood in the light of the details of the city-comparison and other details of the discussion. In this regard it is again noteworthy that apparently this account of justice as psychic harmony shouldn't be interpreted as only aiming to show the value of justice as a means to a good life. Rather, the purpose is presumably also to clarify more generally the sense in which justice instantiates or exhibits goodness, and to make it recognizable as something good in itself.

Regarding the place of *Republic* among Plato's works, *Republic* (with the exception of Book I) is generally regarded as a Middle Period dialogue. (Justice is also discussed at length in the earlier *Gorgias*.) This means that the views put in Socrates' mouth might not be those of the historical Socrates. They may be Plato's own attempt to develop Socrates' views. Socrates was probably not committed, for instance, to the metaphysics of forms, or the tripartite structure of the soul. The idea that there are moral experts such as the philosopher-rulers who are justified to impose the principles of reason on citizens perceived to possess reason to a lesser extent also seems out of character with other things Socrates says. Plato's thought here seems to be that if the people's own reason isn't powerful enough to rule them, then the rule of reason is to be imported from outside, so to speak, with the important thing being that reason should rule. This idea of moral experts, however, seems not to fit very well with Socrates' insistence that each person needs to discover philosophical and moral knowledge for themselves. (*See*, SOCRATES, APPLIED ETHICS.)

Further reading

Annas, J. (1981), *An Introduction to Plato's Republic*. Oxford: Oxford University Press.

Irwin, T. I. (1995), *Plato's Ethics*. Oxford: Oxford University Press.

Plato (1961), *Republic, Gorgias*, in Hamilton, E. and Cairns, H. (eds.), *The Collected Dialogues of Plato*. Princeton: Princeton University Press.

John Rawls, *A Theory of Justice*

Rawls' *A Theory of Justice* from 1971 is a highly influential discussion of social JUSTICE that addresses the question of how society should be organized in order for it to be just. (A revised edition was published in 1999; references are to the latter.) The goal of Rawls' theory is to determine the principles governing just social institutions, or the basic structure of society. This means determining the appropriate way for such institutions to distribute RIGHTS and duties (or the benefits and burdens of social cooperation) to the members of society. In this way the theory seeks to describe what a well-ordered and ideally just society would be like, whereby a well-ordered society is one regulated by a public, shared conception of justice. By contrast, actual societies are typically not regulated by a public conception of justice. Their members have different conceptions of justice and thus what is just is in dispute.

Regarding the importance of justice and the task of determining its principles, according to Rawls, 'any reasonably complete ethical theory' must include principles for society's basic structure that constitute a doctrine of justice (TJ, 9). And as he emphasizes, 'Justice is the first virtue of social institutions, as truth is of systems of thought' (TJ, 3). This means that, regardless of how efficient or well organized, for example, a system of laws is, if it isn't just, it must be reformed or abolished. Rawls' statement also brings to view a contrast between his theory and utilitarianism, which at the time of the publication of his book was the dominating ethical theory and to which his theory offers an alternative. For, insofar as something less than justice would lead to a greater balance of happiness or utility, that is what the utilitarian theory would prescribe. Utilitarianism therefore doesn't treat justice as something inviolable, unlike Rawls' theory. (*See*, CONSEQUENTIALISM, *UTILITARIANISM*.)

Rawls characterizes his theory as an attempt to carry to a higher order of abstraction the traditional theory of social contract represented by John Locke (1632–1704), Rousseau and Kant. To this end, the theory organizes relevant philosophical views into a general framework and clarifies their central idea by using certain simplifying devices – most notably, the notion of a hypothetical situation of equality and IMPARTIALITY under which the contract is determined (see below). It is this notion of a contract that also puts Rawls in a position to maintain that the principles of justice are both inviolable and unconditional in this sense, and yet don't have an *a priori* status. That is, conceived as an object of a hypothetical contract, the principles of justice emerge as something fixed 'once and for all' and 'in advance' but nevertheless not determinable through mere conceptual analysis or a Kantian transcendental philosophical inquiry. Rather, Rawlsian hypothetical agreement on the principles of justice rests on knowledge of general empirical facts about human nature as well as those of external nature. Hence, with the help of his notion of a contract, Rawls seems able to account for something like Kantian unconditionality of moral principles, but to avoid the metaphysical burdens of Kant's theory. Moreover, in accordance with Kant's notion of autonomy Rawlsian principles too are freely chosen. 'The original position may be viewed as a procedural interpretation of Kant's conception of autonomy and the categorical imperative within the framework of an empirical theory' (TJ, 226). (*See*, KANT, GROUNDWORK.)

The basic idea of Rawls' theory is captured in his notion of justice as fairness. The suggestion isn't that justice can always be understood in terms of fairness. Instead, like traditional social contract theories, Rawls' theory envisages the principles that determine the basic structure of a just society as the object of an agreement or a contract. Here 'justice as fairness' then means that the conditions under which the agreement is arrived at are fair. As Rawls states, the principles are ones that 'free and rational persons concerned to further their own interests would accept in an initial position of equality as defining the fundamental terms of their association' (TJ, 10). More specifically and with respect to Rawls' aspiration to clarify the insight of contractual theories, it is important that his theory involves no claims about anyone (in the past, present or future) actually agreeing on a contract or that an actual contract should constitute the basis of society. Rawls is fully aware that we are normally born into society, and his goals are philosophical or clarificatory, not political. That is, the aim isn't to establish an actual political order, but to determine what an ideally just society *would* be like. It is in this sense that the notion of an agreement reached in an 'hypothetical situation of equal liberty' or 'original position' constitutes the heart of Rawls' theory. The hypothetical agreement determines what counts as just and unjust, but only in the sense of fixing a certain conception of justice and defining the terms of cooperation *in principle*. Similarly, Rawls maintains, the notion of the original position can be used to determine the concept of moral right or other virtues besides justice. In this sense the moral philosophical relevance of this notion or procedure extends even further than the identification of the principles of justice.

Thus, although Rawls does indeed aim in *A Theory of Justice* to establish certain principles of justice, his notion of a contract and a hypothetical situation of agreement is 'merely' a philosophical expository and justificatory device. The notion of a hypothetical situation in which the principles are determined is a device of abstraction from current circumstances in society that serves the purpose of enabling us to determine principles that would be truly just. Rawls describes the original positions as follows:

> Among the essential features of this situation is that no one knows his place in society, his class positions or social status, nor does anyone know his fortune in the distribution of natural assets and abilities, his intelligence, strength and the like. I shall even assume that the parties do not know their conceptions of the good or their special psychological propensities. (TJ, 11; cf. 118)

Thus the principles of justice are chosen behind a veil of ignorance, as Rawls puts it. The veil ensures that these principles are the result of a fair agreement in that, provided that no one knows their positions, abilities, and so on, the parties can't design the principles so as to benefit from them at the expense of others. Knowledge of all particularities that would enable them to do just that (as opposed to knowledge of relevant general facts) is excluded. Accordingly, the hypothetical situation of agreement might also be characterized as ensuring the IMPARTIALITY of the choice of principles. In a situation such as the original position, rational persons – whereby rationality means narrow economic rationality of choosing the most effective means to a given end – are assumed to end up with principles that best serve all, even though they act purely from self-interest and are entirely disinterested in others' interests. The veil, so to speak, neutralizes personal interests and turns them into shared, impartial interests that privilege no one in particular. (*See*, IMPARTIALITY.)

Given that no actual contract is assumed or intended, the point of contract-terminology is that the notion of what rational persons would choose and agree upon can function as a way to justify and explain particular conceptions of justice. Particular principles of justice can be regarded as justified insofar as they would be agreed upon by rational persons in an initial situation of equality. Accordingly, the justification of actual social arrangements can be examined in the light of whether they could have been arrived at through such a sequence of hypothetical agreements. This is the sense in which the original position constitutes an expository and justificatory device. More specifically, it can be understood as spelling out the limits of fair terms of social cooperation. According to Rawls, the ideal outcome of the hypothetical contract would be that it determines a unique set of principles of justice. If it fails to determine such a set, his weaker hope is that it still makes possible the ranking of the main traditional conceptions of social justice. In this regard, Rawls is especially concerned to argue that the principles that would be chosen would not be utilitarian.

As Rawls seeks to demonstrate, the original position would lead to the adoption of two principles. The first principle requires equality in the assignments of basic rights and duties; the second holds that social and economic inequalities are just insofar as they result in compensating benefits for everyone, especially the least advantaged. In other words, that some earn greater benefits is just, according to him, insofar as this improves the situations of the less well-off. According to Rawls' first formulation, the principles are as follows: (1) '[E]ach person is to have an equal right to the most extensive scheme of equal basic liberties compatible with a similar scheme of liberties for others.' (2) '[S]ocial and economic inequalities are to be arranged so that they are both (a) reasonably expected to be to everyone's advantage, and (b) attached to positions and offices open to all' (TJ, 53).

Here the point of the first principle is to ensure that everyone has maximal FREEDOM to pursue their aims and their conception of GOOD, whatever that might be. All that is known behind the veil of ignorance is that there will be such goals and conceptions, but not their specific content. Nevertheless, to ensure that the members of society can pursue their aims and conception of good, it seems rational to adopt the principle of equal liberty, which also includes, for example, the liberty of conscience and religion. According to Rawls, the first principle has priority over the second one in the sense that liberty can't be exchanged for any other goods, unlike utilitarianism would suggest wherever restrictions on liberty allow for a greater balance of welfare. But once the principle of equal liberty is accepted in the original position, it can't be taken back. To interfere with liberty on any other basis than the principle itself allows for would be interfering with justice. In this sense the precedence of liberty means that it may be restricted only for the sake of liberty. (*See also*, FREEDOM.)

The second so-called difference-principle ensures that, starting from a position of equality, any differences between individuals are such that they benefit the less well-off. This also provides a way to justify the differences to the less fortunate. Notably, however, when talking about well-offness, the concept of good is presupposed in a sense that is defined independently of the principles of justice or right agreed in the original position. Good in this sense of a 'thin theory', as Rawls calls it, is defined as an object of rational desire. A good object is one that possesses properties that it is rational to want in an object of that kind. Accordingly, a good life for a person would be one lived according to a plan it would be rational for that person to desire, given her endowments, inclinations, and so on. Here a relevantly specified life plan specifies a person's conception of good and sets a standard by reference to which the extent to which she has achieved happiness can be determined. (Differences of endowment, and so on, between persons also explain how a good life can be different for different persons.) Nevertheless, for Rawls the concept of right remains primary in the sense that something can be good solely insofar as it fits into ways of living that are consistent with the principles of right determined in the original position. On the other hand, once the concept of right has been determined by employing the notion of the original position and relying on the thin theory of good, the concept of good can then be defined in a more comprehensive manner. In this way the scope of the theory can be further extended.

Besides having influenced philosophical discussions of justice more than any other work produced in the twentieth century, Rawls' theory has also – inevitably – invited various criticisms. Some of these criticisms are discussed in the section on JUSTICE.

Further reading

Mandle, J. (2009), *Rawls's* A Theory of Justice: *An Introduction*. Cambridge: Cambridge University Press.

Rawls, J. (1999), *A Theory of Justice* (revised edn). Cambridge, MA: Harvard University Press.

—(2001), *Justice as Fairness: A Restatement*. Cambridge, MA: Harvard University Press.

Detailed List of Sections

Index